MW00833917

IF YOUR WIFE KICKS YOU OUT GRAB THE FRIDGE AND RUN!

ROB COPE

Copyright © 2016 Rob Cope

All rights reserved. No part of this publication may be reproduced
or distributed in any form or by any means without the prior
written permission of the author.

Editing, cover design, and book layout by Kevin Miller

ISBN: 978-0-473-35290-5

CONTENTS

DEDICATION

To my children Jaya, Xavier, and Phoenix.

May you always challenge everything I and the world teaches you. Cut your own path through life, for there is no "right" way. Each of you are so gorgeous and unique and have gifts that the world needs. Find them, embrace them, and when I'm an old man, sit beside me and tell me of all the mighty adventures you have had along the way.

1

"I NEED YOU TO LEAVE."

Those are the words I awoke to on my eighteenth wedding anniversary.

Some days, I wonder if any of this is actually real or if I'm just an eighty-year-old man with Alzheimer's dreaming. That day was one of them. I prefer our fifth anniversary, which involved dinner in the Eiffel Tower. Such a better memory.

In all honesty, I didn't see it coming. I thought I was going to get laid. Birthdays and anniversaries, right? Guaranteed sex days for the married man. This was the woman I loved and adored, and her words cut me to the core.

But this is not a story of depressing tragedy. It's a story of triumph and freedom, figuring my way through the wilderness of divorce, cutting my own path, and ignoring what others thought of my attempt to stay sane.

My way of coping with such a huge loss? I grabbed my fridge, and hitchhiked more than 4,500 km around New Zealand.

This is my story.

2

MY LIFE AS A SCREENPLAY

Always start with a good quote:

"The reason we struggle with insecurity is because we compare our behind-the-scenes with everyone else's highlight reel." —Steve Furtick

Have you ever had one of those days that seem like something straight out of a movie?

November 5, 2013 was one of those highlight reel days. If my life were written as a screenplay, that day would read something like this.

                                        FADE IN:

EXT. ROAD OUTSIDE A SMALL TOWN - DAY

Rob, a forty-year-old, bearded man with shoulder-length hair, stands on the road next to a full-sized fridge.

He holds his thumb out to the oncoming traffic.

Approaching cars slow down, puzzled looks on the faces of those passing.

A car pulls over ten meters up the road. Rob runs up to the car as the driver winds down his window.

                    DRIVER
          You smoke weed?

Rob gives the car a once over. It's old and full of house-painting gear.

                    ROB
          Yeah sure, but I don't
          Think my fridge is going
          to fit.

                    DRIVER
          What fridge?

                    ROB (V.O.)
          You think I would have
          learned by now. Note to
          self: Dudes on drugs
          don't see fridge. Got it.

                    ROB
          That fridge back on the
          side of the road. I'm
          hitchhiking around the
          country with it.

A smile comes over the driver's face.

                    DRIVER
          You're hitchhiking with
          A fucking fridge?

                    ROB
          Yes, sir, I am.

                    DRIVER
          Well, I can't bloody
          take that with me, can
          I?

                    ROB
          No, I don't think so.

The driver reaches under his seat and brings
out what looks like a two-pound bag of
marijuana. He grabs a handful, and gives it
to Rob.

                    ROB
          Wow. Thanks.

Rob sniffs it, smelling its potency.

                    ROB
          That's some really strong
          stuff. I don't suppose you've
          got a pouch or something I
          could put this in, do you?

                    DRIVER
          Do I look like a fucking kangaroo?

The driver floors it, leaving Rob with a
handful of a few days in prison.

                    ROB
        Shit.

                    ROB (V.O.)
        But hang on. This isn't
        the day. Fast forward a
        week.

EXT. SIDE OF ROAD - DAY

Rob stands on the side of the road surrounded
by farmland, his thumb out. A pickup pulls
over, and a couple of farmers jump out. They
talk for a minute before throwing the fridge
on the back.

INT. TRUCK - DAY

The farmer in the passenger seat turns around
and looks at Rob, dead serious.

                    FARMER
        You start talking about
        Jesus, and I'll throw you
        straight back on the road
        again.

He passes Rob a beer. Rob accepts it with a
grin.

                    ROB
        So you don't want me to
        tell you about the good
        lord then?

                    ROB (V.O.)
        This isn't the day
        either. Fast forward

one more week

INT. PRISON CELL - NIGHT

Through the bars, we see a man asleep on the top bunk. A gorgeous, dark-haired, olive-skinned woman lies on the bunk below. Her head is thrown back in passion and partially buried by her arm as she bites her bottom lip, her naked breast visible in the moonlight. A man kisses down her stomach as her body shudders with desire.

The action freezes.

                    ROB (V.O)
          No, wait. This was the
          end of my day. Earlier that
          day, I found myself waking up
          in Christchurch for the first
          time. A city that had been
          destroyed by an earthquake more
          than two years earlier and was
          still in ruins.

INT. HOUSE - MORNING

Half-awake, Rob stumbles to the bathroom in his underwear.

                    CAROLINA
          Remember to only piss in
          that toilet. The plumbing's still
          busted. And if you need to
          really go, it's a twenty-minute
          walk down the road to the public
          loos. Or you can go in a plastic bag.

                    ROB
        You serious?

                    CAROLINA
        Oh yeah.

INT. KITCHEN - LATER

Fully dressed, Rob leans against the kitchen
counter sipping a coffee as a small handful
of other people buzz around getting ready for
the day.

                    ROB
        Any chance of a lift into
        the main city with my fridge this
        morning?

                    CAROLINA
        Sure thing. John's heading
        There in about half an hour.

                    ROB (V.O)
        It was at that point, after my
        coffee that I realised I really
        needed to go. I mean, really go!
        And the twenty-minute walk to the
        public toilets was not an option.

Rob searches around and finds a bucket and a
couple of plastic bags. He double-bags the
bucket and then heads to the toilet. Moments
later, he reappears with the plastic bag in
hand, knotted at the top.

                    ROB
        Where do I put this?

Everyone looks at him in disbelief. Then they break into laughter.

                    REBECCA
        Well, you told him to...

A sheepish look comes over Rob's face.

                    ROB (V.O)
        Was I the butt of a bad joke?
        I didn't know. I mean, the
        Toilet was busted. Fuck.

                    CAROLINA
        That's all right. Go throw
        it in the bin. The bins
        around here were full of
        shit for the first year
        after the quake.

Rob heads to the outside bin, holding the bag at arm's length as everyone makes way.

                    ROB
        Shit.

EXT. CHRISTCHURCH INNER CITY - LATER

Rob unloads his fridge from the back of a 4x4 and stands surrounded by blocks of rubble and vacant lots where high-rise buildings once stood.

His cell phone rings.

                    ROB
        Hey, Rob here.

                    GREG (O.S.)
          Hi Rob. It's Greg from *Seven
          Sharp.* I heard you were in town.
          We'd like to do a piece on you
          tonight for our show.

Camera zooms out to fly over scene, showing
Rob standing next to his fridge on the phone
in the midst of a broken city

EXT. JAILHOUSE BACKPACKERS - DAY

It's an old 1800s prison that has been
converted into a backpackers' hostel.

INT. JAILHOUSE BACKPACKERS - DAY

Rob checks in. Leaves his fridge in the lobby
and heads upstairs.

The rooms are old prison cells with heavy
steel doors and bars on the windows. The
cells line the exterior walls of the building
with an open mezzanine to the floor below.
With the exception of fresh paint and carpet,
it is the same as when it was used to house
convicts for more than 125 years.

INT. ROB'S CELL - DAY

Rob puts his backpack on the bottom bunk and
takes it all in. His bunkmate for the night
enters.

                    ROB
          Hey man, I'm Rob.

                    BUNKMATE
          Hi. I'm Thor. Nice to meet
          you.

                    ROB
          Thor? That's a great name.
          Where are you from?

                    THOR
          Denmark.

                    ROB
          Nice! The Nordic god of
          Thunder as my roommate, in
          an old prison cell.

EXT. SIDE OF THE ROAD - DAY

A camera crew prepares to interview Rob.
GREG, the producer, counts them down.

                    GREG
          And we're live in 3, 2...

INT. BURGER KING - LATER

Rob sits eating a burger, his fridge by his
side. He's receiving text after text from
friends from all over the country who have
seen the show.

His cell phone rings.

                    ROB
          Hey, Rob here.

                    WOMAN'S VOICE (O.S.)
                      (French accent)
          Hi Rob. It's Lorena. We met in
          Murchison two weeks ago.
          Do you remember me?

                         ROB
          Hell yeah, I remember you.
          How you doing?

                       LORENA
          I'm great. Some friends just
          told me they saw you on the
          side of the road with your
          fridge in Christchurch! I'm in
          Christchurch. Do you want
          to have a drink?

                      ROB (V.O.)
          Are you fucking kidding me?
          I'd met this goddess of a woman
          on the fourth night of my tour
          and thought she was amazing.
          And now she wanted to go out
          for a drink? Hang on a minute.
          Let me think --

                         ROB
          Yes!

                      ROB (V.0)
          Recap of day so far. Shitting
          in a bucket, prison cell with
          Thor, prime time national news
          coverage, Burger King, and now
          a drink with a gorgeous French
          girl.

EXT. PUB - NIGHT

Lorena and Rob enjoy a drink and a smoke, the conversation filled with laughter.

> BARTENDER
> The bar's closing in ten minutes.

> ROB
> Shall we head down to the next one?
>
> LORENA
> That would be great!

EXT. STREET - NIGHT

The two walk along.

> ROB (V.O.)
> Just going to fast-forward this to the best part.

Fast forward visually as they hit the next pub, drink, leave, get a bottle of wine, and sit talking and drinking outside the prison. They kiss.

INT. ROB'S CELL - NIGHT

They enter, and Thor is asleep on the top bunk. The two lie there looking at each other as they start to make love.

> ROB (V.O.)
> The perfect day.

FADE OUT

Making love to a beautiful French girl in an old prison cell under the Nordic god of thunder. What a contrast to the pain and torment of the previous few months, a journey that had begun with those fateful words: "I need you to leave."

If I'd known then where my life would head over the next couple of years, maybe those words wouldn't have had the same bite, but at that time and place, those words were like a sword to my soul.

This is where I'll start my story.

Rachel, my marriage, I really thought we were going to make it. I really did.

In the end, the same forces of nature that drew us together also tore us apart.

3

THE BEGINNING

Rachel, the love of my life for more than twenty years.

It was always her. She was all I ever wanted, from the first moment I saw her until that day a lifetime later when she spoke those words that ripped me in two and I found myself standing on the side of the road with a fridge.

We were sixteen. She was gorgeous, full of life, and the only person who believed what I believed with the same passion and zeal. By nineteen, we were together, and I was about to head out on the road with my band for a year of touring.

Back then, both of us were extremely religious. It would not be an understatement to say I was a Christian zealot. Although agnostic now, in my late teens, I rose at four in the morning to pray for two hours before reading my Bible for an hour. I was driven to please God to such an unhealthy extent that by the time I was twenty, I was a burnt-out, suicidal mess.

I was the singer in the band. We had started in high school, and now we were taking on the world. Every gig we played, I gave it my all. By the end of each gig, I usually couldn't talk, because I'd left my voice on stage. I loved it, loved the passion of yelling into a microphone, of connecting with the audience. Being in that space is one of the greatest feelings in the world. It's where the purest aspects of my personality and passion collide.

Some weekends, I'd hitchhike back to Hamilton to see Rach for a day before having to hitch back for a gig somewhere in the country come Monday. These were the days before texting, email, and Facebook, so we wrote each other every week. I'd tell her where I was going to be, and she'd post something to the local post office where I was heading. All those letters are still around here somewhere.

Six guys in a van travelling the country, living on almost nothing, sleeping wherever people would let us crash, completely broke but entirely alive. It was one of the best years of my life.

But it came at a heavy price.

Burnt out from leaving myself on stage every day, I spent the next few years in darkness, suicidal, then numb.

I was lost.

Unable to do the band thing anymore, I returned to Hamilton to be with Rachel. I needed to find work and try to get on my feet, to find some sense of stability.

After a few months, I found work, and a year later, we were married. However, for the first two years of our marriage, I was still completely burnt out. I was numb. Couldn't feel a thing, not even for Rachel. I couldn't laugh, couldn't cry. I felt nothing. That's when most people would have left, but Rachel hung in there. I guess she had seen me at my best, seen my strength, and although a total mess now, hoped that I'd get my mojo back one day. And I did—ten years later.

For those first years of our marriage, I worked long, hard hours starting my own construction company, which kept my mind off all the other stuff. Rach finished her degree and began her teaching career. We both loved kids, but we wanted to travel the world first, so we did. What started out as a two-year trip ended up being nearly six.

We obtained working visas for Canada and landed in Vancouver. Bought a big Dodge van and drove for three months with some friends all over the United States. From Vancouver, we headed to London, where we worked and travelled for nearly four years before going to Rwanda for six months to fulfil Rachel's childhood dream of working with kids in Africa.

We had this desire to help each other fulfil our dreams, and that's exactly what we did.

The whole time we travelled though, I was in mental turmoil. Throughout my twenties, I'd been struggling to recover from burnout, struggling to figure out who I was and where I fit in. How could I get my mojo back? I was depressed and then angry, prone to flying into rages at the drop of a hat, and I wouldn't last at any job for more than a few weeks.

I had some beliefs that were still killing me. It's amazing how one or two beliefs can completely cripple someone. I wrote about this in my first book, **Men Wanted for Hazardous Journey.** Here's an excerpt.

Dodgy London flat and my unholy mantra

London, 2001. I'm lying in bed in our dodgy Willesdon Green flat. It's only four degrees inside, because our "bedroom" is actually a conservatory with a thin plastic roof. I shiver as I ready myself to get up and face the day. Cue the record in my head that I so loved to begin with each new morning: **"Useless, bloody useless!"** That had been my dad's throwaway comment cast in my direction many years earlier in moments of frustration. Now it had become my unholy mantra, and I believed it.

I believed it, because that's how I felt, "useless, bloody useless," and I felt that way, because when I compared myself to everyone around me, that's what I saw.

What I didn't realise then is that I was comparing myself to the facades—the masks of others rather than their true selves—and that I didn't truly know anyone at all, let alone myself.

My idea of manhood was to get a job and work hard, because that's what all the men in my family did. My dad was a workaholic, but that wasn't me at all. I was a dreamer, an actor, a zealot.

I had done my fair share of work by then. I had even started my own one-man construction company. While travelling, I could easily find work as a carpenter on highrise buildings. But inevitably, I would come home depressed that I wasn't following my passions.

So I would quit my job and follow my dream of becoming an actor. After all, I was in London, and there was no better place to pursue that dream. Then I would get a part in a play (which paid little to nothing) and beat myself up that I wasn't "working." I wasn't doing what a man is supposed to do—bring home the bacon. My wife was doing that.

I also had a lot of dreams, big ideas about how to make the world a better place. I would spend hours writing these ideas down and working out how to make them happen. Like an artist with a paintbrush and an empty canvas, I would fill pages with my designs, plans, and structures, only to be struck down by fear, the overwhelming sense that I was just too lazy or not really skilled enough to make them happen.

I was also tormented by some of my religious ideals at the time, which told me "God has a plan for your life." Every time I started towards a new plan or goal, these beliefs would pin me to the wall. "Are these your plans, God, or is it just my ego and should I surrender it all to You?" I would cry out before falling into yet another pit of despair.

At this point you're probably thinking I had a couple of screws loose. And you're right, except I couldn't see that my beliefs were killing me. I lived in the darkest of places and had no idea that wasn't normal.

By then, we were in our late twenties and headed back to New Zealand to start a family.

We ended up in the little beachside community of Algies Bay north of Auckland. With the help of my parents, who put their home up as security, we were able to buy a section, and I built our first home. And what a home! I had finally succeeded at something.

It was a huge, two-story house with curved ceilings, sea views, massive decks, and a two-bedroom apartment downstairs we could rent out. Best of all, like my father and his father before him, I had built it with my own two hands.

We moved in just in time for the home birth of our first child, Jaya. Then the property market went crazy, and our home doubled in value. I had my mojo back, and all of those years of what felt like failure were finally behind me.

At that time, I also began some serious counselling. I didn't want to pass my shit on to my kids. I didn't want to be that angry arsehole of a dad I was heading towards becoming.

A couple of people had told me about this guy David Riddell, a counsellor who was so skilled that a one-hour phone conversation with him was a game changer. I usually don't believe that kind of hype, but I booked my phone appointment anyway. It was a six-week wait. Okay, I figured, he must be good. Six weeks later, I called him, and sure enough, he nailed me. Within the hour, I was undone.

David was very direct. He would dig, dig, dig like an old school surgeon looking for cancer. Here it is, and here is how you need to cut it out. As a guy, this was exactly the approach I needed. Just tell me how to fix the fucking thing, and then give me the tools!

I did a lot of self-work. Not only had I found the best counsellor, I studied under him to get as many insights into my beliefs and behaviours as possible. I got a lot of my shit together over the next two years. My anger subsided, and my rage all but disappeared. I had insights into my depression and found the tools I needed to deal with it.

It's interesting to write this down and have the revelation as I do so that the two people who have helped me the most in my life are two very wise and highly skilled counsellors. These guys have dedicated their lives to helping people find truth and insights, and I'm forever grateful.

During that time, I was also continuing with my acting career and was starting to get a few good roles on different TV shows, something I'd been pursuing for years.

These were the golden days before the storms of life tried to drown me.

4

I'm Untouchable!

I thought I had the Midas touch. Over the past couple of years, nearly everything I touched turned to gold. Plus, my mental health was the strongest it had ever been. I had my mojo back in spades. I was reading a lot of books, trying to get deeper insights. M. Scott Peck's *The Road Less Travelled.* Viktor E. Frankl's *Man's Search for Meaning.* I also read books on property and making money, I challenged and stretched my understanding of everything: spirituality, religion, parenting, the human condition, money. I was a sponge for knowledge and deeper understanding.

Until then, I'd never given a fuck about money, but I started to see it as a tool for me to pursue greater dreams, so I chased it.

I eyed up five acres of undeveloped land at the top of our street and, through reading these books, learned how to get options to buy the property from the owners. We sold our home and pocketed over $300,000. With the options on the land in place, we bought a section that would give us access to develop the land behind. I was on fire!

However later that same week, the local council changed their bylaws, and the purpose for which we bought the land was made redundant.

Frustrated but not deterred, I found another entrance point and obtained an option to buy. I had geotechnical surveys done and subdivision plans drawn up and got as far as having a buyer lined up for the whole project, which would see us pocket around $2 million, except... I'd missed a major covenant on part of the land. Long story short, the whole thing fell over, and we lost everything.

We ended up living with Rachel's sister and her four kids at the other end of the country in Naenae Lower Hutt for the next eighteen months as I tried to get back on my feet. By then, we had our second child, Xavier, so all together, there were nine of us living in this small house.

I was so desperate I went door-to-door asking people if they wanted free landscape designs in an attempt to create work and pay some bills. Out of all the days knocking on doors and doing the hard yards, I landed one four-hour job.

In the meantime, I was trying to put property deals together.

The market had crashed, and property was cheap, so I knew I could make money if I had the right partner.

I pushed and pushed until a chance conversation with one of Rachel's best friends from childhood led to a massive breakthrough. (He was also a really good friend of mine, as I'd known him through Rach for fifteen years by then.) He had started to make good money with his company and loved the idea of property, but he didn't have the time or the skillset to do anything about it. So we were off. He financed everything, and I found the property to buy, renovate, and rent out.

We started a company, but because Rachel and I were still facing the forced sale of the land up north and possible bankruptcy, we decided it was best, for borrowing purposes, if we were just silent partners with a side joint venture agreement, an agreement that I never signed—another harsh lesson to come.

With this partner, we bought $1.2 million in property, and I increased the value to over $1.5 million with a passive income of $600 per week. Everything I'd learned in these books told me I should find more partners and do more deals, so that's what I did. Within two years, I had traded more than $6 million in property using no money of my own (because I didn't have any!).

For much of this work, I just made a good finder's fee, enough to pay the bills, because my eye was on the long-term goal of the properties we held as rentals, the properties for which I had never signed the joint-venture agreement, the properties that our "good friend" decided he wanted all for himself.

When we received the letter from his lawyer, I felt like I'd been hit by a truck. I asked my lawyer about the worst-case scenario. He said we could be fighting through the courts for a couple of years, and if I lost, I would have to pay my ex-business partner's legal fees on top of my own. Two years of bitterness. I couldn't think of anything worse. For the sake of my mental health and my family, I let it go. I ate a fucking shit sandwich.

By that time, we were living in one of the houses we had bought and renovated with my ex-partner and paid "rent" each week into the company we had started, even though our names were not on the ownership documents.

We stopped paying the rent until this whole matter was resolved. Because of this, he took us to the tenancy court. Two weeks before Christmas 2011, we and our—now three—children were court-ordered out of our home with nowhere to go. We were homeless.

This was the pile of bricks that broke Rachel. She was never the same again. The betrayal of a good friend and another self-induced, catastrophic financial failure was too much.

Two years later as I stood in the ruins of my marriage she said, "Life with you is like being on a roller coaster, and I need to get off."

God, I wanted to be bitter, to hate. I felt so justified. But I'd seen what bitterness did to people, rotting them slowly from the inside. I'd seen how it darkened the souls of even the brightest among us. The only way to fight bitterness was to find an insight into my ex-partner's behaviour and own my part of the business failure. Why hadn't I finalised and signed the JV agreement? Why had I trusted him to such a huge degree without putting in some protection?

One of the greatest lessons I've ever learned is that I'm not a victim. No matter what happens, I still get to choose how I respond. But this was a hard one. Betrayal is hard to deal with. It took me more than two years to find the insight I needed to even start forgiving my ex-business partner.

I choose to forgive for me, because it sets me free. I've got one life to live, and I don't want to waste a minute in hatred.

5

STABILITY VS. SECURITY

Rachel needed stability and security more than ever, so I tried to provide it. I'm a self-employed builder. I've been self-employed most of my life. This means I have lots of work, and then no work, which, of course, also means lots of money and then no money. To me, this seems like the natural flow of things—summer, autumn, winter, spring, and on it goes. Apples don't grow all year round. I've always lived in the tension of these seasons, and I don't want to live any other way.

Rachel, on the other hand, has always been an employee. Employees knows the hours they will work and the income they will receive. I couldn't live like that, always knowing, a world with limited possibilities. I need to live in a space of endless possibilities. But I was willing to give it a good go if it would help her out. If it would save my marriage.
I couldn't bear the idea of working in my trade for someone else, working twice as hard to earn half as much and

nowhere near enough to cover the bills.

Finally, I found a role I could go for. It was for the regional coordinator of Big Buddy, a charity that connects good men with boys who don't have fathers in their lives. This was right up my alley and was in line with my own charity, Project Wildman, which is based around getting guys to start talking about the real shit in life.

I was one of two hundred people who applied for the position. I passed the first round and then the second. There were police checks and long interviews with family members and friends. These guys were thorough!

Finally, it was down to one other guy and me. By that point, for the sake of my marriage, half of me was hoping I'd get the job, but the other half of me realised that the majority of this job would involve sitting in an office by myself doing paperwork. I dreaded the idea.

This was a rare moment in my life when I was not being true to myself, and I was doing so to please someone else. I felt it deep down. I knew if I got the job, it would slowly leach the life out of me, and I'd end up in a dark place.

Oh, the sweet relief when the phone call came and they said they had given the job to the other guy!

It had taken me years to figure out who I was and what I was passionate about and to accept myself for me, to not measure myself by other people's standards. I had risked losing myself to save my marriage. It was a powerful reminder to never lose myself again.

6

I'm Not "the One"

In the doorway of our bedroom stood the woman of my dreams, the woman with whom I'd spent the past twenty years and hoped to spend the next forty.

"I need you to leave."

Was she joking? She didn't look like she was joking.

Over the next few months, I was faced with the reality that my wife did not love me as I loved her, that I wasn't "the one." I wasn't her "soul mate."

Anger, denial, bargaining, depression, I knew what I was about to face. "It's not that bad," I kept saying over and over. (This would be called denial.) I couldn't see how our marriage was that bad. It wasn't awesome, but to end it? Really? It's that bad?

In my mind, I had a picture of women leaving guys because they were abusive or unfaithful or drunks. I was a thousand miles from perfect, but I wasn't a scoundrel. I was genuinely trying my best.

I turned to anger, a friend I knew all too well, and blamed Rachel for her part in it.

This turned to bargaining. "Okay so how do we make this work? What can I do? What can **we** do?"

All this time, I was trying to put into practice everything I'd learned over recent years about respecting other people's stories. Although in pain, a big part of me totally respected the strength it took Rachel to end it. Knowing what this meant for the kids and the pain we would all be facing, she was being authentic, and I admired that.

Our family backgrounds are completely different. Rachel's family has always lived by the motto "peace at any price." Don't be honest in case it hurts someone. My family is the complete opposite. We say it as we see it regardless of whether it hurts someone. So, despite how difficult it was to hear Rachel say those words, this was the authenticity for which I'd been waiting.

That said, as I write this, I can see that my anger when we

were younger had taught her that I wasn't a safe person with whom to be honest. I was never physically violent; that's not my nature. Verbally, yes, and living with me in my twenties and a large part of my thirties must have been pure hell. I hated myself so much back then that I couldn't handle being loved by someone. Whenever Rachel looked at me with eyes of love and admiration, I felt such a sense of panic that I'd sabotage it every time so that she would hate me, a feeling with which I was much more comfortable.

A few years before our separation, once I'd healed a lot of that, we were lying in bed just looking at each other, her with those big doe eyes totally in love with me. "Years ago, you would have sabotaged this," she said.

Boy, that's hard to write.

Even after I finally worked through a lot of my shit and learned to love myself, we still managed to miss each other. Our love languages were never in synch. My first two love languages are touch and words of affirmation. I would show her love the best way I knew how, encouraging her, kissing her, cuddling her, making love. But oftentimes when I showed love this way, she felt like I was taking from her, because her love languages were completely different from mine. Hers are quality time and gift giving. I never want and rarely give gifts; they mean nothing to me. Yet, that is how she needed to be loved. Quality time I could do, take her out to a café and talk, but she needed that more than I could give and vice versa.

Two people trying to make it work, trying to love each other and yet missing each other completely, because we were speaking two entirely different languages.

Family mottos, beliefs, self-love, self-hatred, loss of trust, intimacy and connection, love languages . . . so many variables to try and make something work

These days, women file for three out of four divorces. That's a lot to think about. Why is the balance so far out of whack?

7

How Do I Leave?

Rachel needed me to leave, but I couldn't do it. I didn't know how a "good" man should respond to such a request. Was I supposed to just get up and leave because she asked me to? Or should I stay and fight for my family? I decided to stay. And fight.

Because I wouldn't leave, Rachel saw me as selfish. I didn't see it that way. This was my family, after all, my kids. It wasn't like I was a guest who had overstayed his welcome. This was my home. I kept telling her she was more than welcome to leave if she needed space. After all, that's what I would do.

I went through so much pain during this time that I'm still struggling to get it out.

Loving someone who doesn't love you the same way back is one of the harshest of realities to come to terms with.
We decided to try to make it work. We owed that much to

ourselves and the kids. We went to counsellors and tried to see where we were missing each other, what we could do to find middle ground.

I didn't like her counsellor, and she didn't like mine.

My counsellor, David, is very direct and always brings it back to what you can change in yourself. I was used to owning my shit. I'd spent the past ten years doing it. I would talk to David and figure out my stuff and what I needed to change, and Rachel would talk to her counsellor.

A big thing that was never fully addressed, and yet was also a key factor, was how we parented our children. As many couples do, we tried to raise our kids in a way that is nigh impossible to pull off by two people and actually requires an entire tribe.

Over the past decade, I had watched this beautiful woman slowly burn herself out trying to live up to her ideal picture of motherhood. The same "all or nothing approach" I'd taken to religion twenty years earlier, which had leached the life from me, had ensnared Rachel in terms of motherhood.

She was a schoolteacher and had worked in early childhood education and as a nanny, so I was more than happy to follow her lead through parenthood.

All of our children were born at home, and I loved that. With the exception of Jaya, our first, we didn't have any scans while they were in utero in case of . . . I can't remember why. And no vaccinations.

Rachel breastfed on demand 24/7, and they all slept in our bed for the first couple of years, which I also loved. I hated the idea of my kids crying themselves to sleep in a room all alone, and I loved waking up to them all snuggled into me in the morning.

This was the kind of parenting I wanted to do, but it came at a high price. Rachel and I had little time for "us." When we could, we went on a date night for a couple of hours, and there were periods when we managed to make that a solid routine. But then our next child would arrive, and it went out the window once more. For nine years, we never even had a single night away together. Like a garden starved of water and sunlight, our marriage had been dying for years under the savage taskmaster of idealism.

With the exception of the above major oversight, I think it's fair to say that over the next three to four months, we both gave it a good shot. I was full of optimism that we would get through it, but slowly, things grew dark.

The final straw came after she had seen another counsellor

who had her write out a list of the top five traits she needed in a life partner, and none of those traits described me.

I was so angry at that list. Only one of them was something on which I could work. The other four were personality traits that were the exact opposite of me. It felt like she'd bought a fridge twenty years earlier and was disappointed now that it wasn't washing and drying her clothes.

In retrospect, I don't think Rachel was asking me to change who I was. It was more of a realization in her mind that I could never be what she needed me to be, so why go on?

My Marriage is Over

Over the next few days, I called a good mate, Richard, and went down to the pub for a catch up.

"She's right, our marriage is over," I said an hour into our talk as a wave of shame washed over me and I struggled to hold back the tears. I was in a pub after all, and men don't cry in pubs. Certain rules of manhood must be followed.

Rachel was right. I needed to leave, but I needed to do so on my own terms.

Before I made the final call, I talked to David one last time.

"So you're not willing to give up who you are in order to save your marriage?"

"No, I'm not."

"Well, there's your answer then," was his wise reply.

I went home and talked to Rachel. "I'll give you what you want. I'll leave. But I need to do it on my terms when I've figured a few things out."

I'd seen a lot of mates go through this, and nearly all of them had wound up in a one-bedroom apartment depressed and drinking themselves stupid. After what I'd fought to break free from in my twenties, there was no way in hell I was going down that dark path of depression again. I needed to get out of Dodge. I needed to do something wild, to feel the wind in my hair. I needed a hazardous journey with endless possibilities. I needed to do something mental in order to stay sane, but without leaving my kids for too long.

I knew that if I got my head straight, then my kids would suffer a lot less. I didn't want this to turn me into a hurt, angry, and bitter man. That's not how I wanted my kids to see me.

So many ideas rushed through my head. Go to Australia and work in the mines. The Cook Islands. Ah shit! What about jumping in my van and driving around the country promoting my book?

Over the past few months, I'd written and self-published my first book, *Men Wanted for Hazardous Journey,* which was a look at Kiwi man culture and the unspoken rules by which we live.

Yes! Now we're talking. But alone in a van? I could go for months without having a conversation with anyone, and I knew that part of my journey needed to be talking with people to process and grieve.

What about hitchhiking? Yes. That way I'd be forced to connect with people. But just hitchhiking wasn't enough. I needed to put an obstacle in my way. My book was called *Men Wanted for Hazardous Journey,* so I wanted just that, as hazardous a journey as I could create.

I thought about all the inanimate objects I could take, but everything kept coming back to the idea of a fridge, because there's nothing funnier than a fridge, and I needed some humour in my life right about then.

The idea wasn't even original. I had read Tony Hawks' book,

Round Ireland with a Fridge, years back, where he had done just that with a small beer fridge as a drunken bet. It was a great read, but the idea wasn't even original to him, as the bet arose after witnessing an old Irish man trying to hitchhike with his fridge.

So, a fridge it was, but a full-sized one. After all, I live in New Zealand, the land of meat-eating, beer-drinking, rugby-playing hard men, and everything here needs to be man-sized. I didn't want guys to be able to say, "Why don't you get a real fridge?" Instead, I wanted the response to be, "How big is the fridge? A full-sized fridge/freezer? That's fucking awesome!"

And awesome it would be. On November 1, 2013, I packed my fridge, dropped my kids at school, kissed them goodbye, and headed to the ferry that would carry me across Cook Strait to begin the first leg of my journey.

8

HITCHHIKING . . . WITH A FRIDGE

I rocked on up to the ferry desk with my fridge in tow feeling like a proper dick and asked for two tickets, one for me and one for my fridge.

In truth, I was shitting myself.

"You can't take a fridge on board," the lady behind the counter replied.

"Well, I have to," I said. "I'm hitchhiking around the country with it."

Eyebrows lifted. Looks were given. Then came the inevitable smile that became the response of most whom I would encounter over the next few weeks. After a bit of discussion with managers and shipping staff, it was decided I could get it on board as cargo in the cargo hold.

Sorted.

That afternoon, I arrived in Picton, a small port town at the top of the South Island, and made my way to a backpackers (hostel) for my first night.

I had the fridge on a trolley so I could push it around from place to place. As I walked the streets of Picton, people gave me every look you can imagine. I still felt like an idiot.

A couple of days earlier, I had decided to stay in backpackers along the way. I didn't like the idea of isolation, sleeping alone in a tent, and I couldn't afford hotels, which would have also been isolating.

What's funny looking back now though is that on my first night, the staff put my fridge and me in a room with six beds and no one else. I hadn't had any media coverage at that stage, so I guess the question at the time was, "Is he mentally challenged?"

The answer, of course, was "yes."

Little did I realise I was about to discover something very important about New Zealand backpackers: they are full of gorgeous European women.
I spent the first night talking to and enjoying a few drinks with

travellers from all over the world. Not only were they gorgeous, they were also happy. It was their big overseas experience and they were in New Zealand, *Lord of the Rings* country. What's not to be happy about, right?

I woke early the following morning, made my coffee on the little stovetop espresso maker I had packed in my fridge, and hit the road.

Nervous, terrified, stupid, broken, uncertain, lost, all of these emotions bombarded me as I walked the fridge to the outskirts of town to look for my first hitching spot.

Hitchhiking is all about the right spot—well, that and looking the part. You have to be where people can see you, where the cars are driving slow enough so that drivers have time to look you over to assess if you're safe. And the fridge definitely complicated things.

"Is that a fridge? Why does he have a fridge? What's in the fridge? Is he a serial killer? Is there beer inside? A body?"

I knew all of this, and my mind was buzzing. I felt like quitting before I even started.

After twenty minutes of pushing the fridge, I found the right spot and stood there a moment before finally putting my thumb out along with my giant, friendly, "I'm not going to kill you" hitchhiker's smile.

People looked and looked again. Some looked angry, like I'd invaded their sense of reality with complete nonsense. Others looked in disbelief, their jaw dropping as their brain tried to reconcile what they were witnessing. Others just grinned from ear to ear like this simple bit of madness had made their day.

I liked this last group. It turned out that hitchhiking with a fridge is a great filter, because only the hard case, slightly mad but totally fun people picked me up—either them or those who were on drugs.

Within ten minutes on that first morning, an old dude pulled over to give me a ride. A small problem arose. The fridge was fucking huge!

As I stated earlier, I wanted to make this trip hard, all or nothing. Also, I needed a fridge big enough to fit all my stuff. It was like a giant, waterproof backpack filled with my clothes, food, sleeping bag, tent, pillow—I love my pillow, such a hard man—and, of course, copies of my book, which I planned to sell along the way.

Fully packed, it weighed about 80 kg, and my body felt it

those first few days. My arms were covered with bruises as I learned the best way to get it in and out of vehicles.

There I was, my first offer of a ride, and I had to decline. But someone had stopped! Maybe this would work. I had had visions of being stuck in one place for days on end, and there I was being offered a ride within ten minutes. Pure gold!

The old guy drove off, and ten minutes later, I had another offer, but once again, my fridge was too big.

Third time lucky? Yes! A young guy, Ben, driving a 4x4 pulled over and lowered the passenger window.

"What ya doing with the fridge, mate?"

A question I'd get used to answering soon enough.

"Just hitchhiking around the country with it."

"Sweet."

He jumped out of his truck. After unloading his dog and a few chainsaws, we lifted the fridge into the back, repacked everything, dog included, and we were off.

My first ride sorted!

During our half-hour drive, we talked, exchanged stories, and I was reminded of another great thing about hitchhiking that I'd forgotten from earlier years thumbing my way around the place. People talk about real stuff with brutal honesty. It's kind of like, "Well, we're both complete strangers and will never see each other again, so I'm going to just say it as it is." These conversations along the way became one of the most healing parts of my trip, just hearing other people's stories and being reminded every day that we are all in this life thing together. Trying to figure it out, who we are, where we fit and how to make it all work.

I had already experienced a lot of this over the previous two years. In 2011, I had set up Project Wildman, which has a straight shooting raw structure and an environment for guys to drop the bullshit masks and just be honest about life. By the time I started my fridge tour, I had five groups running weekly in Wellington, where I lived. I had my own group of about ten guys, and we met every Tuesday night around the fire. I would also go and sit with the other groups every now and then to see how they were going.

For the two years leading up to the end of my marriage, and then through the eventual break-up, I had about forty guys whom I had started to get to know really well. Forty guys with forty different perspectives on everything.

Some had been married forever. Others had been through several marriages or long-term relationships, while others were true bachelors. They were from all walks of life, backgrounds, and professions. What this meant for me was that I saw a bigger picture, that there is no "right" way to deal with something like a divorce, and what's right for one person may not be right for another.

So, with forty different perspectives, I cut my own path. I didn't follow any rules or programs. My way of coping with the end of my marriage was to grab the fridge and run. But even this was not a pain-free experience. Within the next couple of days on the road, I would find myself standing at the gates of hell.

After Ben dropped me off in Blenheim, I waited in the blistering sun for two and half hours before being picked up by a doctor on his way to the bush for a couple of days. I love New Zealand!

He dropped me in Havelock, where I waited for a while before an energetic guy pulled over and offered me a ride. "Can you help me get the fridge in the back?" I asked.

"What fridge?" he replied.

First warning sign . . . ignored.

He sees the fridge. "Oh, you've got a fucking fridge! Throw it in. Let's go!"

So we did, and off we drove.

It wasn't long before I realised this guy talked fast and nonstop. I deduced this by the way that he talked—fast and non-stop. His driving was also somewhat . . . erratic. Sweet as, it's only a two-hour drive!

"I do a lot of speed," he said finally.

"No shit."

"Do you want a bump?"

Such a generous guy, offering me his drugs.
"Nah, I'm all good. Cheers, bro."

It was at that point I accepted death as a real possibility if I was going to hitch over 4,500km. This, however, did not mean I had a death wish.

Two hours later, we arrived in Nelson, and he drove me right up to the backpackers. Hell of a nice guy. Stop doing drugs and driving!

I don't know why I chose that hostel. Maybe it had something to do with the pool, sauna, spa . . . Once again, I met a great group of people and had an amazing time. Except, this time I found myself sitting at a table in the early hours of the morning playing a drinking game that I didn't fully understand and having to down a full mixed pot of every drink under the sun. Not my brightest moment. The next day I was fucked. That was my day at hells gate.

A good Scottish friend of mine, Hamish, whom I call "McSqizzy," had been part of my Wildman group in Wellington. Now he lived in Tasman with his young family. He was picking me up that morning to take me to his place for the night. Meanwhile, I'd never felt so hung over in my life. I was beyond miserable.

I spent the day "sleeping" on his couch as his kids ran around the place being kids.

As I lay there, I was on the verge of a full mental breakdown. The big low after a big high the night before. Seeing my good mate and his family still happy and together while I had just lost mine made me wonder what the hell I was doing with a fucking fridge!

It felt like I was balancing on a razor's edge. I could either tip into madness or find the resolve to get up and get on the road again. This was my self-induced hell as the sadness of everything I had lost hit me over and over again like a man trying to stand in the surf while the ocean is in storm.

I don't know how I did it, but I got up the next morning and found the road again. I think part of it was lack of options. "What else do I have?" I asked myself. "It's either this madness or go back and find that deathtrap of isolation in a one-bedroom apartment and drink myself stupid every night." I also saw that drinking that much in Nelson had been a massive trigger and that I wouldn't pull the trigger that hard again.

So, there I was on the side of the road once more, struggling desperately but also knowing I had to keep going no matter how hard it was.

One, two, three hours and no rides. And then a car full of young guys pulled up, and they all piled out of the car.

"Dude! We've seen you all over Facebook! You're a fucking legend."

Wow, I thought, ***that's pretty cool.***

"What you're doing is inspirational. I want to do some crazy shit like that," one of them continued. Just what I needed to hear. I thanked them for their encouragement and gave them a copy of my book. I was filled with newfound enthusiasm.

A short time later, my cell phone rang. It was Boris from **The Nutters Club,** a New Zealand radio show that deals with mental health. He had read my book and was keen to have me on the show when I got to Auckland. Wow! Where was all this coming from?

Soon enough, I got another short ride, and then another and another. I ended up at the Lazy Cow backpackers in Murchison for the night.

I was still tired from the drunken fiasco a couple of nights earlier, so I headed to my top bunk for a bit of a nana nap.

Before long, I heard the sound of a beautiful French voice coming from the lounge asking whose fridge was sitting in the hallway. Now, I've always had a thing for French women—the accent, the passion, the love. . . . Too many movies. But my curiosity was sparked when I heard this voice asking about my fridge!

I jumped out of bed and tried to act all casual as I entered the room.

"Hey, how are you doing? I'm Rob, and this is my fridge."

What a great pickup line.

"We saw you today in Richmond," she exclaimed.

I had seen three people hitchhiking about a hundred meters up the road from me earlier that day. They were dancing around all happy, trying to get a lift.

"That was us," she exclaimed with a giant grin on her face. And what a face! She was gorgeous! Dark skin, dark hair, dark eyes. So fucking French.

"Why are you hitchhiking with a fridge?"

"Oh you know. . . . " I was still trying to act all cool.
The truth was, I didn't know how to talk to women as a single guy. I'd been with the same woman for so long I was well out of practice. My role model for talking to girls was actually my oldest son Xavier, who was six years old at the time. He was a real smoothie.

I remember seeing him at school when he was only four going up to a girl in his class and saying, "That's a lovely dress you've got on today," and then she melted into his arms. Holy crap! Where did this kid come from?

So, that was my model: be honest and authentic and speak

from the heart. Say what you see. That's usually how I talked to most people anyway. Oh, that applies to hot French women, too? So much to learn.

That night, Lorena (the French girl), two German guys, an Israeli, and me sat around talking, laughing, playing guitar, and having a great old time. Every time I looked at that goddess, I thought, *I need to make love to you.*

9

ON THE ROAD AGAIN

"You smoke weed?"

Those were the first words to fall out of this guy's mouth the following morning as he pulled over to give me a lift.

Earlier that morning as I got ready to leave the Lazy Cow, I'd made Lorena an espresso from my little travel coffeemaker of awesomeness before hugging her goodbye and telling her I thought she was absolutely gorgeous, just like my son had taught me. I was being honest. And now some stoned-out dude was asking me if I smoked weed. Not my usual start to the day.

Recap of story from intro of book: Big handful of weed, the driver wasn't a "fucking kangaroo," and I was standing there wondering what to do.

So, I pushed the fridge off the road and wandered back to

the Lazy Cow. Lorena and the others were sitting outside enjoying the sun. I walked up to her, and as "a parting gift," I placed the pot on the table right in front of her.

"No way!" she exclaimed with that great accent that drives me crazy.

I told them the story. She hugged me goodbye again, and I left once more to go and stand with my fridge. Two minutes later, a cop pulled up, and I quietly thanked the gods.

Over the next couple of days, I hitched my way up and around Westport and down the west coast past Punakaiki, Greymouth, and Hokitika. My fridge and I were well into the flow of travelling, and the dark days of Nelson and Tasman that nearly ended me were well behind.

I'd stopped and done a couple of interviews about my book and travels for radio as well as local papers. More people were hearing about my adventure, and they were keen to know more.

I was hitching out of Greymouth one day when a little old lady in her eighties named Claris walked past.

"I heard you on the wireless this morning, my dear," she said. She was lovely, and we talked for a while. She even signed my fridge, and I gave her a big hug before she continued walking along the route she had, no doubt, walked a thousand times before.

I had chosen to tackle this route down the west coast first, because it's one of the most isolated parts of NZ, and if I was going to get stuck anywhere, it would be there. Usually, I had to wait two to three hours for a lift, but if I was in the right spot, sometimes I'd get a ride within minutes. However, I was about to do the stretch between Hokitika and Wanaka, which is more than 400 km of wild coastline and rainforest.

My first ride out of Hokitika confirmed my fears when a well-intentioned older gentleman on his way to get free firewood from a deserted logging road dropped me in a hitchhiking black spot. Yes, it was still on the main road, but it was in the middle of nowhere on a 100 km/hour stretch of road with only about a foot or two of shoulder on which to stand. What made it even more interesting was that the layout of the road meant that most cars couldn't see me until they were right on top of me. The good news was, it was only two in the afternoon, which meant I still had seven hours of daylight. A little mantra that helps me stay sane in such moments kicked in: "It is what it is." In other words, there's nothing I could do to change the situation, so why stress about it?

An hour went by.

It is what it is.

Two hours went by.

It is what it is.

Two and a half hours.

Oh, come on!

Then another older gentleman pulled over. "That's a terrible place to hitchhike from."

"Tell me about it," I said. We threw the fridge on his truck, and off we sped.

He dropped me in a small town with a garage, a pub, and a few houses scattered around the place. He knew the guy at the garage, who was just about to close up for the night, and told him what I was doing. They discussed where I could sleep if I got stuck.

Eventually, I wandered down the road a little and found my hitching spot—right outside a house two doors down from the pub. I stood there with my fridge and my thumb out as vehicles passed by every two to three minutes.

Before long, an old man working in his front garden appeared. He looked at me, and I waved. He ignored me, and I felt like a right idiot again.

I hadn't been there long when a tour bus came cruising down the road. I put my thumb out for every vehicle, even motorbikes, because it always made me laugh, so I did the same for tour buses, not actually expecting a ride. To my surprise this bus pulled over, and as the doors opened, another scene from my movie life unfolded as a busload of beautiful European women poured out. They gathered around me, smiling and laughing.

I looked over at the old man in his garden, a stupid grin plastered all over my face while my fridge and I were loaded onto the bus. He had his head down, shaking it in disbelief. As we sped off, I imagined him going inside, unplugging his fridge, and dragging it to the side of the road to try his luck.

Over the next couple of days, I worked my way down the west coast, getting stranded a few more times and having little adventures along the way. There may have even been an incident involving a courier van and a tray of beautifully iced muffins that may or may not have accidently been sprawled all over the parcels, van, and driver. Sorry, Matt!

And then I hit Wanaka. I love Wanaka!

Wanaka is an amazing little lakeside village surrounded by snow-capped mountains and breathtaking scenery. Add to that the sleepy, laid-back nature of the place with just enough cafes and pubs to keep it comfortably social, and in my book, you've got paradise. I'd forgotten how much I loved that place. Upon arrival, I decided I'd definitely spend a couple of days relaxing there.

I checked into the Purple Cow backpackers. What's with New Zealand and cows? Then I rested up for a bit in my six-bed dorm.

As I mentioned earlier, one of the most appealing things about backpackers is the diverse range of people you meet from all over the world. My dorm at the Purple Cow was no exception. There was an Indian guy, a Chinese guy, a Swedish girl, a German girl, and Mohammed, a Pakistani carpet salesman who would roll out his mat, face Mecca, and pray right in the middle of the room. I liked Mohammed. We were both around the same age. He was also a father, and he worked hard to provide for his family while travelling the country.

A year later, at the same backpackers, I met him again on my second fridge tour. We even wound up in the same room together! The next day when I left Wanaka to hitch to Queenstown, Mohammed and his business partner took a corner too fast in icy conditions and were killed on the same road I had travelled only minutes earlier. It was a sharp reminder of how short life is. My heart went out to his family.

For the moment though, I was enjoying relaxing in Wanaka for the day. I took the fridge for a walk to the waterfront and talked to a few people, including an American guy who exclaimed in his booming voice, "Didn't we see you yesterday down the west coast in the middle of nowhere?"

"Yes you did. Thanks for the lift!" I said with a cheeky smile.

"Oh, we just thought you were selling whitebait on the side of the road."

We cracked up laughing. For some here in New Zealand, whitebait, a tiny transparent juvenile fish about an inch or two long that run once a year, is a delicacy. There's a limited season in which to catch them, so people go crazy over them for a couple of months. Up and down the west coast during this time, many conversations inevitably come back to the baby fish.

People sell it on the side of the road and out of the back of cars. Others make egg fritters with them to sell. As long as you don't look at the fish, with their little, black beady eyes, they actually taste pretty good.

That night at the backpackers, I was in the kitchen cooking dinner. By then I'd learned that the kitchen was the most social place to be and by far the best place to meet people. Plus, I love cooking.

I got talking to a Canadian girl, Myrinda. Just your usual, "So where are you from? How long have you been travelling NZ?" before she asked me why I was in Wanaka.

"Did you see that fridge out there in the entranceway?"

"Yes I did," she said with a heightened sense of curiosity.

"That's mine. I'm hitchhiking around the country with it."

She stopped what she was doing and looked at me. "Well, you just got a whole lot more interesting, didn't you!"

"Oh, I'm awesome," I replied. "Did I not mention that yet?"

We ended up talking for hours over a couple of bottles of wine before heading down to the beach with another bottle to share.

It felt so good to connect on such a deep level with a woman. I love connecting with people like that. Back in my real life, I usually spent my days working alone or with other guys, and in the evening I would do Wildman, which was with guys once again. So this was great, a night alone connecting with a beautiful woman.

In the early hours of the morning, as we headed to bed, we gave each other a really long, deep, "right down to my soul" kind of hug. All was good in the universe.

The next morning, I was all packed ready to leave for Queenstown when Myrinda gave me a jade necklace from British Columbia, her home province. It was a parting gift for the beautiful night before. It was awesome, and I wore it for the next few months as a reminder that I could connect with incredible women, that there was hope for the future.

I headed to Queenstown for the night before working my way further east. I was heading into farming country. I stood on the side of the road once more, the sun on my face and feeling full of hope and fluffy bunnies.

It didn't take long before these two "cockys" (what we call dairy farmers in NZ) pulled up in their pickup truck and the whole "You start talking about Jesus and you're straight back on the road again" incident happened, followed by the downing of a couple of beers as we sped along.

It really is like they say, "You only rent beer." It passes straight through me.

I was busting for a piss. The cockys dropped me off at the far edge of a small town, which would usually be great, except there was nowhere to relieve the growing pressure. I looked around desperately but found nothing!

Five minutes later, a lady and her daughter picked me up. She said she could take me all the way to Invercargill, my destination for the day, but it was an hour away. Usually, I would have been happy for such a ride, but how was I going to hold on for that long?

An hour of great conversation mixed with desperation as we travelled through the farming country of southland.

I grew up in the Waikato in the middle of the North Island, which is similar farm country. One time when we were kids, my sister and I were playing with some friends down on the farm that our home backed onto when one of her friends became desperate to pee. My sister, who had a cruel sense of humour, informed her friend that if she touched the electric fence, she wouldn't need to pee anymore.

My sister's friend, obviously a trusting soul, listened to this sound advice and proceeded to reach out and grab the wire.

Wallop!

I don't know if you've ever touched one of those fuckers, but they carry 10,000 volts, and they kick! Needless to say, the girl was lying on the ground covered in her own piss while my sister stood there laughing. "Well, ya don't need to go anymore, do you?"

I was kicked a few times back then, too. One time I was out collecting field mushrooms mid-autumn when the growing conditions were perfect. Clutching a bowl of them, I ducked under an electric fence on my way home with my bounty.

Wallop!

All I remembered was waking up spread-eagled on the grass with mushrooms everywhere. It must have clipped me on the back of the neck and knocked me clean out.

But that was nothing compared to the day I was attacked by a fence that nearly left me dead. This story is kind of embarrassing, because I was about twenty-two years old and should have known better. I was doing some work around the home of a farmer when, for some reason I no longer can remember, I had to get across a field that had an electric fence in the middle of it. I decided the best way through this one was over it, so took a big run up and tried to jump it. I say "tried," because what actually happened was that my boot got caught on the bottom wire, which also collected the top wire as I fell over the fence, and my foot was trapped between both of them, which were twisted together as I lay on the other side.

Panic set in. The thing about electric fences is that the 10,000 volts is not constant. It pulses about every two to three seconds. I hit the ground and . . . Bang! I tried to stand up. Bang! I lay there with one foot in the air entangled in this fence, which was kicking me with 10,000 volts every couple of seconds. I tried to stand up again and again, and each time the fence knocked me to my arse!

The headline "Worker found dead trapped in electric fence" raced through my mind.

Bang! On the ground again.

Okay, I thought, trying to control the panic, *this is a timing thing. The only way out of this is to jump back over. Wait for it* . . . Bang! Now up and over . . . No! Bang! On the ground over and over until I finally got my timing right and landed back on the other side of the fence.

Freedom!

I lay there for a few minutes recovering from my near death experience before finally getting back to my feet and looking around, hoping no one had seen it. Holy shit!

Now, where was I? Yes, sitting in the back of a car with my fridge heading to Invercargill busting for a piss, and for some reason thinking about electric fences.

Finally, we arrived, and they were generous enough to drop me right outside the backpackers. I got the fridge out and ran to the front door, only to find a note: "Back in ten minutes."

Fuck!

I looked around desperately for a bush, hoping I wouldn't get caught mid-stream with the owner's arrival. Oh, sweet relief as I emptied two bottles of beer onto his plum tree.

Up early and on the road the next morning, it didn't take long before a young lady pulled over and asked if I'd been to Bluff yet. Bluff is the southernmost town of the South Island, and her offer of a ride there and back was too good to refuse. We did the trip, got the photos, and an hour later, I was in the same spot trying to hitch north. Hitchhiking out of Invercargill with a fridge can be a real mission!

Two, three, eight hours passed. It was a hot day in the

blistering sun, and no one was stopping to give me a lift. People **were** stopping, however, to encourage me. People stopped for a chat and gave me food and drinks and ice cream! Amazing hospitality for sure, but no rides.

Eight and a half hours. I was so tired! Do you know how much energy it takes to smile the hitchhiker's smile for that long? It was fair to say that by five thirty, I was fucked.

I was just about to give up hope for the day when an old dude towing a trailer pulled over. "You're standing in the wrong spot, mate. You need to be a couple of miles down the road."

"Don't suppose I could throw the fridge on the trailer and get a lift down there, could I?"

"Sure thing!"

Eight and a half hours—two miles travelled.

I was on the outskirts of town, in the "right spot," and the right spot it was! Within thirty minutes, I was out of there and got dropped in the next town twenty minutes up the road.

From there, I waited another half hour before I caught another lift to Gore, another twenty minutes up the road.

Ten hours, forty minutes travelled. Awesome.

The following morning, after another couple of hours standing on the side of the road, I was out of Gore and on my way north again.

As we drove, the couple who picked me up told me their story. They had lived on neighbouring farms for twenty years and eventually fell in love, left their partners for each other, and were really happy together. They pointed out their old farms as we drove by and they recounted the story.

Every day, I heard real life stories from real people—the good, the bad, the tragic, and the bizarre. It was all helping me to heal from the loss of my own marriage as I was reminded constantly that we are all human, all trying to figure our way through this life, that life throws most of us a few curveballs, and how we deal with these plot twists reveals and defines our character.

Would I sit in the pain of this, in hurt and blame, bitterness and unforgiveness, festering away, or would I own my part in it, heal, and move on?

A couple of rides and a few more small town newspaper interviews later, I hit Dunedin!
Dunedin was good to me—very good, in fact. It was the

beginning of some major media coverage, starting with making the front page of the *Otago Daily Times,* followed by an interview on Dunedin television and an interview with Jim Mora on his nationally broadcast radio talkback show. By the time I left Dunedin three days later, it seemed like everyone knew who I was and what I was doing. In fact, I didn't even need to put my thumb out to get a ride out of the city. A couple of guys just pulled over and yelled, "Hey fridge guy, do ya need a lift?"

Further up the line on my way to Oamaru while I was in a small town waiting for a ride, a girl from a fish and chip shop walked out with a big feed of fish and chips for me.

"Here you go, fridge guy. Good luck!"

Wow!

Oamaru.

Now, I didn't really know anything about Oamaru before I got there. I thought it was a small nothing South Island town that was kind of dull and dying. Boy was I wrong!

I arrived right in the middle of their Victorian Fete. The town was buzzing with men, women, and children dressed in old Victorian costumes while others had fully embraced the

Steam Punk movement. Old guys and girls walked around carrying ray guns doing their thing and having a great old time. Oddly enough, my fridge and I fit right in.

I love the old Victorian quarter, where some people make their living as they would have done two hundred years earlier, spending their days handcrafting furniture, book binding, stone carving, and whiskey making. There's even an old Penny Farthing shop where you can hire one of these old, crazy looking bikes that was run by an old dude who had ridden the length of NZ on his giant wheeled contraption. The streets were alive with bike races and stone cutting races, dancers, and old steam-driven tractors, cars, and trains. Talk about stepping back in time!

I checked into the old Imperial hotel/backpackers and got talking to the couple who ran the place. I gifted a copy of my book to the guy, who returned later that night to say, "Dude, it's like you've written my life's story in that book. Thank you!" It was a response I heard a lot more over the following year as I sold more and more books and guys started to realise that, as men, we have a common story of disconnection and that maybe it's time to talk about it.

I headed back out to the celebrations with my fridge and met a fantastic selection of strange, fun, and interesting people, one of whom was a nineteen-year-old guy who called himself

"Wild-boy."

Wild-boy, a.k.a. Brando, had an interesting story. He was an Auckland guy who had decided he didn't want the life he and his mates were heading towards with the drinking and drugs, so he started an epic journey to walk the entire coastline of NZ, living off the land as he went. By the time I met him in Oamaru, he was already ten months in.

I admired this young man immensely. He was actually doing something, carving his own path in life, initiating himself into manhood. By the time he completed his trip, he became the first known person in history to walk the entire coast of New Zealand. Better yet, he had become a man on his own terms with a foundation that will last him a lifetime.

My own initiation into manhood had also taken place when I was nineteen when I toured with my band. The importance of this journey into manhood is undervalued in our society. It's a rite of passage, a breaking free from parents and societal structures to claim our own unique path and live on our own terms.

I guess that's part of what the fridge tour was for me twenty years later: finding my true north again. Having been in the structure of marriage for so long, I needed something big, mad, and adventurous. There were no rules. I was free, and

I felt it.

I read an article recently that said the same thing, that one of the best ways to get over a long-term relationship is to travel, because one of the hardest parts to deal with is the loss of what's normal, routine—coming home to an empty house each night rather than being greeted by your partner, eating dinner alone rather than sharing a meal, spending weekends alone, etc. Travel removes all of that, for a time while you go out and explore endless possibilities and are reminded just how big the world is and how many fascinating and amazing people inhabit it. It's like a kickstart in a new direction. Whether that direction is right or not is beside the point. In fact, I don't know if there is a "right" direction. It's a time of complete chaos where the world is tipped on its head and everything is arse about face. For me, however, I think there were wrong directions. The worst would have been bitterness or no direction at all, just sitting there waiting for the tide to drown me.

Fuck that shit!

The fridge and me at Cape Reinga, the top of New Zealand

Random kids signing my fridge in Queenstown

The lovely Claris signing my fridge in Greymouth

Boys in blue stopping to buy my book

Christchurch in ruins from the earthquake

Lake Wakatipu

My days of off-line dating — T-shirts
courtesy of my workmate, Jason

Best ride ever in a '65 Impala

My kids helping me get ready for the second fridge tour

First Leg

SOUTH ISLAND OF NEW ZEALAND

Second Leg

10

EARTHQUAKE-STRICKEN CHRISTCHURCH

I hadn't seen Christchurch since the enormous earthquakes that had destroyed it and taken the lives of 185 people two years earlier.

After a long day on the road from Oamaru, I made it. A woman named Carolina driving a tour bus picked me up in Ashburton and let me crash at her depot for the night with a group of other drivers.

That night, I talked to Rachel on the phone for about an hour. I had left knowing it was over, but she was still the woman I loved. Rachel told me she had found a place, and when I got back from the tour, the house would be empty.

I pleaded with her not to throw away twenty years. I was still hanging on by my fingertips, hoping against hope we could make it work. Later that night, I received a text from her saying, "I need to do what's right for me," and that was it.

It hurt like hell, but at the same time, I understood it. She needed to cut her own path, too, to find her own way, and I wanted to respect that no matter how much it hurt.

I'd been on the road two weeks by then, but Rachel and I, although still living in the same house, hadn't been together for a good couple of months.

Yes, I'd been flirting with women over the past couple of weeks, but only flirting. This conversation finalised things for me though. Tomorrow, my entire world would change.

Christchurch: The opening movie scene of this book unfolds. The shitting in a bucket, national TV, the jailhouse, and making love to Lorena the French girl as my roommate Thor slept blissfully unaware on the bunk above us.

The morning after, Lorena and I, having only had a couple of hours' sleep, made love again. The truth was, I hadn't really slept at all. I lay there most of the night just looking at this gorgeous woman as she lay sleeping in my arms with a big smile on her face, lit by the moonlight pouring through the cell window.

My mind tried to reconcile this complex mixture of pure

elation and deep grieving that was taking place at the same time. Making love to another woman was my way of ending my marriage for certain and moving on, but it was also so much more.

I always thought I'd be the guy who waited a couple of years before being with another woman. To my way of thinking, that was the mature thing to do. But it turned out that intimacy and connection had been in deficit for so long that this was the first thing I sorted out. The fact that being with a beautiful French girl had always been a dream of mine and that the first woman after my marriage ended was just that still blows my mind, like some kind of gift from the gods.

Over the next couple of days, I thought about Lorena all the time as I worked my way north. We messaged each other constantly, and it was becoming clear that we had connected in a stronger way than either of us had thought at first.

"I want to make a crazy love story with you," she said.

Her words were exactly what I needed right then. Oh, to be wanted once more.

By the end of the week, after more crazy rides, awesome people, and even a crayfish dinner, I was back on the ferry heading home to see my kids for a few days before starting the second leg of my journey.

11

HALFWAY

Rachel hadn't moved out of our house yet, but we had arranged for me to stay for the next four days with the kids while she headed off to her sister's.

It was great to see my children again. I told them about some of my adventures and gave them the gifts I had bought hurriedly in Picton only hours earlier when I remembered, *Shit, kids always need gifts after a trip away.* They were tourist gifts from a tourist shop, but they loved them.

Those few days flew by, and once again, the time came for me to head off. I dropped the kids off at school, and then a mate picked me up and dropped me a few miles up the road in the right hitching spot.

It was a Monday morning, and I couldn't help but notice how depressed everyone looked as they passed me by, long, sad faces bombarded my happy space as I stood there waiting.

I'd had that exact face many mornings in my life as I headed to work contemplating some of the shit jobs I would facing that day. But not that day! And not for the next three weeks!

Before too long, I had been picked up, dropped off, picked up, and dropped off again before being picked up by Jason, who was heading all the way to Palmy, my next stop!

There are two cities in NZ that I really struggle to appreciate fully: Hamilton "the Tron" and Palmerston North or "Palmy." I'd lived in both of them, albeit twenty years earlier, but they felt the same as I remembered them, a dull heaviness in the air and the threat of street violence simmering just beneath the surface.

Ten years earlier, my brother, Steve, who was living in Palmy was getting married, so we threw him a bachelor party. We did some crazy stuff, including holding him down and waxing his arse. Boy, can that guy clench!

After the waxing incident, we dressed him up in little gold underpants, put a snorkel, mask, and diving flippers on him, and walked him through town.

As we headed through the main square, a young drunk guy started yelling at us and wanted to fight my bro, and he wasn't joking!

"Are you having a fucking laugh, mate?" I asked the guy. "Look at him. Do ya think he wants to fight?"

So, there I was, back in Palmy, the land of smooth arseholes, and people looking for fights.

The next morning was my first day in the rain. So far, the sun had followed the fridge everywhere, even down the west coast of the South Island, which is also known as the "wet coast," something to do with it being a rain forest. Nevertheless, I had had perfect sunshine and even managed to get sunstroke. I started to believe that maybe my fridge had magical powers, but Palmy, good old Palmerston North, shattered my illusions!

Rain jacket on, walking down the road, getting soaked. Actually, I didn't really mind, it was all part of the experience. What helped as well was the fact that the messaging with Lorena was getting more and more interesting. For the first time, I discovered what "sexting" was. Wow! There I was trying to concentrate on getting a ride, and I was getting these incredibly sexy messages that were, quite frankly, making my male member stand up and take notice. I literally had to stand behind my fridge a few times and wait for things to subside before continuing.

It turned out that Lorena was heading north from Christchurch to Auckland, so it was decided she'd swing by New Plymouth on her way so we could spend a proper night together without any Nordic gods present. I was so happy. I was like a little boy waiting for Christmas. Only two sleeps to go!

But first, Whanganui.

A group of guys from the Whanganui Stopping Violence group were keen to catch up with me once I hit town. My book and Project Wildman had struck a chord with them, and they wanted to learn more. It was so good to sit down with them and see that many of us are trying to achieve similar things in regards to manhood.

Getting out of Whanganui the next day though was a bit of a mission. There is a big hill to tackle heading north followed by miles of residential housing before getting to the outskirts where my sweet hitching spot would be. Rather than tackle the hill, I decided to try my luck in the city. Two hours later, I was pushing the fridge up the hill as, once more, I learned that mid-city is no place to hitchhike.

The good—no, great—news was that a guy heading in the opposite direction towing a horse float saw me struggling up the hill—it's a fucking big hill—so he turned around, pulled up alongside me, and asked what I was doing. Story told, fridge on board, and he dropped me in the sweet spot on the north side of town. Awesome!

It was a bit of a quiet area with no one around and only the odd car flying by, when, before long, a car heading in the opposite direction caught my attention. It slowed right down as it drove by. It was filled with a half-dozen young gang prospects, and they were all giving me "the look."

Fuck! A lot of violence is involved in the initiation into NZ gangs, and the gang culture in NZ is massive. Standing there, I felt like a slab of meat waiting to be tenderized.

A group of these young prospects often meet about five houses down from where I live in Naenae. I've seen a few of them hobbling around the streets, their faces battered, looking like they've been someone's piñata. In fact, one guy is still limping a year after I first saw him looking that way.

A couple of years ago, I had to call the cops and the fire brigade four times within a month—three times because the violence next door from where I was either working or living got so bad I had to do something and the fourth time when my neighbour's house was burning to the ground. These weren't even gang-related incidents, just the day-to-day underlying tension that exists in many NZ homes.

A few years earlier, when I was living in a really "posh" area, a mentor said to me, "Don't live here. Holiday here, but live where there's life, where the neighbours play their music too loud and piss you off." I wonder if this was what he meant?

So there I was, standing . . . waiting.

Come on, someone get me the fuck out of here! was my constant thought while I waited anxiously for them to come back. The minutes ticked by as I kept my eye on the horizon. And then the ride I'd been hoping for came along, and I was on my way again! I was so relieved—until I realised this latest ride was only heading five minutes north, and I was left standing on the road in an even more isolated area.

Fuck.

Two hours later, I was a little farther up the road when a storm front rolled in. Now, I'm not sure, but I think that a fridge standing on the side of a road out in the open might be exactly what lightning looks to play tiddly winks with.

Shit, what another interesting day, I thought as lightning cracked across the sky and thunder shook the ground.

I arrived in New Plymouth around seven that night. I was pretty tired when my ride dropped me right at the front door of the backpackers but so happy to have made it. The only job of the day that remained was getting the fridge up those thirty steps to my room.

I woke up the next morning to be reminded by my awesome brain that this was the day Lorena was coming!

I booked us a double room with en suite at the backpackers and took off to do a newspaper interview before exploring the city. I really liked that backpackers. It was right in the city with a view of the ocean from the balcony.

That day, I had also arranged to share a meal with Rachel's sister, Maryanne, and her family. I wasn't sure what to expect. I'd known Maryanne for nearly twenty years, and her kids and her husband Ross were like family, but they were family no more. Once again, I was entering unchartered territory and didn't know how all of this worked.

When I arrived at their house, the strange thing was it didn't seem strange at all. In fact, it felt like nothing had changed. We had a great meal, I played with the kids just like I always had, we talked a bit about the divorce, had a laugh or two, and then they dropped me back in town.

"Well, I guess I'll see you on the other side," I said when Ross dropped me off.

"Hey, mate, you've divorced my sister-in-law, not me," he replied.

Nice! I liked that.

Even now, Ross and Maryanne and I still catch up if I'm in town or if they're down here in Wellington. It's the same with my other ex-sister-in-law and her kids. I'm always welcome and vice versa, and their kids are still a part of my life.

Enough of family talk though. Lorena was on her way.
When she arrived, she messaged me, and I walked out to find her. I wasn't sure if it would be weird or not. I had felt a bit weird before she arrived. After all, we had only spent one night together, and what if the spark wasn't there? What if . . . what if . . . what if?

Fuck that!

My life was full of "weird" at the moment, and I'd discovered the best way to tackle the unknown was to walk straight up to it and kiss it in the face. That's exactly what I did with Lorena, walked straight up to her and just kissed her, to which she replied, "Thanks for doing that. I was feeling a little unsure until now."

It was an amazing feeling having this beautiful woman in my

arms again, the touch of her skin, making love. . . .

After a few hours, we left the room and walked along the waterfront to enjoy the sunset before heading back and making love all night while listening to drunk people next door at the local karaoke bar belt out Guns 'n Roses songs.

It had been such a long time since I had felt this way— wanted, desired.

"Romance is all 'yes' and heavy breathing— an affair built around the illusion of unbroken affirmation. Marriage is 'yes' and 'no' and 'maybe'— a relationship of trust that is steeped in the primal ambivalence of love and hate." —Sam Keen.

I knew this quote well, and romance, passion, and lust was what I needed right then.

As soon as Rachel and I started having kids, the passion faded, as it does with many couples. We went from being lovers to parents, and although the connection was still deep for the first few years, it was different.

As I mentioned earlier, we had done what is referred to as "attachment parenting," which means our kids slept in our bed, and we lay down with them as they went to sleep. I loved this style of parenting. I felt, and still feel, so close to my kids because of it, but every bit of energy we had went into the kids, and nothing went into us.

As the years went by, the gap between us as lovers grew bigger and bigger. I had read in Steve Biddulph's book **Manhood** that this is when most marriages fail, largely due to what he calls "the long dark night of the penis." This refers to the fact that, as men, most of us only really feel loved when we are making love. And making love doesn't happen too often when kids are sleeping in the bed.

Back then, I would ask to spend time with Rachel, to make love, but she saw this as being needy. I hated being seen that way. Later, my frustration turned to anger as I felt trapped. I had promised to stay faithful to her, but one of the greatest and most exciting areas of my life had been shelved for too long. Not shelved completely, but I needed sex to be a healthy and regular part of my life.

In **Men Wanted for Hazardous Journey,** I wrote,

> ### It's hard to play second fiddle
>
> As men, when we decide to have a family, we have no idea what we are getting ourselves into. (To be fair, neither do our partners.) We move from a place of freedom to one of responsibility, a place of connection to

one of disconnection and displacement as the children arrive. We are no longer number one in our partner's life, which is a huge and difficult adjustment. For most of us, our partner is the only person with whom we have a strong connection, and when that is temporarily set aside for the sake of the children, we are left with no one.

Although I'm grateful for the way my wife has poured her life into our three children, it has been a hard road learning to live on the scraps of whatever love and affection she may or may not have left at the end of the day. And sex? Sex is seldom, if ever, in the cards. This has been a real place of growing up for me, a place where I have failed miserably on many occasions.

I wanted to grow, to be stretched, to feel loved, to hold onto my family, not lose my family because of my need for sex. But so many times during those years I'd say to myself, "God, I just want to be wanted."

I did grow over those years, and I did stay faithful, but fuck it was hard!

So there I was with Lorena, and for the first time in years, I felt wanted.

This is why I don't think there is any formula for getting over a marriage or long-term relationship, because everyone's journey is different. Everyone's needs are different.

That night at the jailhouse with Lorena, she asked what I wanted most. The first thing to pop out of my mouth was "intimacy and connection."

Today, it still is. That's what I want. That's what I desire, and that's what I seek out.

The next morning, Lorena left for Auckland.

12

HEAD-ON INTO A TRUCK

That day would be another long, hard day on the road as I headed towards Hamilton, my other not-so-favourite NZ city.

I grew up in Huntly, a small coal mining town twenty minutes north of Hamilton. My grandfather, a Scottish immigrant, had worked in those mines to provide for his family.

As a teenager, I had spent many Friday nights on the streets of Hamilton. The street violence I saw and experienced still sat in the back of my mind as I aimed my fridge in that direction and put my thumb out.

Surprisingly, it didn't take long to get a ride, and from right within the city! The ride dropped me in the middle of nowhere, where I had to wait two hours to get a lift to Urenui, a small town that really was in the middle of nowhere.

Before too long though, a lady pulled over and offered me a

ride in her station wagon.

"How far are you going?" I asked, not keen on getting stranded in a dodgy place again.

"I'm not sure yet. I'm just driving," she replied.

Fuck it, I thought and took up the ride.
To get my fridge into her car, we needed to put the back seats down, but we couldn't find a lever to release them.

"It's okay, I'll wait for the next ride," I said.

"Nah, we'll get it," she said and continued to search for another few minutes.

Wow, this lady really wants to take this fridge, I thought.

Finally, we found the lever, lowered the seats, threw the fridge in, and drove off.

Once again, the usual conversation began about the fridge and why I was doing what I was doing. Then I told her about my book.

"What's the book about?"

"It's a look at our Kiwi man culture and how so many of us never really talk about what's going on and then wonder why we're all so fucking depressed and—"

She burst into tears. I didn't know what to think.

"Ya know," the words stumbled out of her mouth, "twenty minutes ago, I dropped my kids at my parents' house, and I've been driving along this road looking for a truck to drive head-on into, because I can't do this anymore. But there haven't been any trucks."

She continued trying to get it out in between sobs. "And then I see you on the side of the road with your big smile, and I just had to stop and pick you up."

"Wow! That sounds like a rough road. You know, if you do it now with me in the car, it will be murder," I said with a cheeky grin on my face.

During my life, I've been in some very dark places, and I related well to her feelings of despair and hopelessness. For me, it had been closing my eyes when driving in the "I don't give a fuck if I die" moments of my life.

I've also had a number of friends who have been to these dark places, and I know that, used appropriately, humour can be a great tool to bring someone back from the edge. I also knew that she wouldn't have picked me up unless even the smallest part of her still wanted to live.

For the next two hours as we drove along, I listened to her story and shared some of my own. We laughed and cried as we recounted some of the fucked-up plot twists life had thrown at us along the way.

By the time she dropped me in the small town of Piopio, we were both feeling lighter, and I knew she was in a clearer head space. After we pulled the fridge from her car, I gave her a copy of my book—and a big hug.

"Thank you," she said before jumping back in her car and driving home. I heard from her a couple of months later via Facebook, and she thanked me again for being the listening ear she needed that day.

I recounted this story during my TEDx talk in Wanaka the following year, a story that choked me up as I relived her feelings of hopelessness that day.

Town hopping was the name of the game for the rest of the day as I made my way, one ride after the other, to the mighty city of Tron.

My family, who still lived in Huntly, wanted to take me out for dinner that night. It was the first time I'd seen them since the break-up, and I wasn't looking forward to talking with them about it. Divorce, although extremely common in New Zealand, wasn't so common in my family, and I was the first one in my generation to go through it.

Six months earlier, my mum had asked me about my marriage to see if we were okay, but I hadn't been in the right head space to talk about it with her. I was talking about it a lot with my Wildman groups, but family was different.

So, there I was that night with Mum, Dad, my two sisters, and my nephews wondering what to say and how much to say. There was still so much I didn't understand. How could I articulate all that was buzzing through my head?

"I wasn't the one," was all I could explain that night.

"It took her twenty years to figure that out?" my mum replied.

"I guess so."

We pretty much kept off the topic for the rest of the night and just had our usual family chat and banter. When the night ended, Dad covered the bill. Nice.

The following morning, I pushed the fridge for about an hour to the northern end of Hamilton before getting picked up and dropped in Huntly. My sister and her two sons popped down to say hello again and get a picture before heading off.

So, there I was in Huntly, my birthplace and hometown, now a forty-year-old man standing on the side of the road with a fridge. I wondered what my sixteen-year-old self would have made of this. I was supposed to be rocking the world by then with my music or be a huge actor or director or something, and there I was with a fucking fridge.

It seems I'd bought into the Hollywood story the same as many others, as I wrote in my first book.

I never made it as a rock star—grieving the fallen hero

In the movie Fight Club, Brad Pitt's character Tyler Durden sums it up best: "We've all been raised on television to believe that one day we'd all be millionaires, movie gods and rock stars, but we won't, and we're slowly learning that fact."

I never made it as a musician or an actor, which were two of my dreams. When I finally accepted this wasn't going to happen, I went through the same process of grieving as I did when I lost my childish view of my father. I needed to be okay with just being me, letting go, and moving on. This was not an overnight occurrence but a slow process that took place over many years. In fact, it's still happening. Today when I hear Chris Cornell or Eddie Vedder belt out a tune on the radio, some of the sadness of never having made it, of just being ordinary, still hits me.

Apart from our shattered dreams, the greatest area of grief today is the loss of our marriages and separation from our kids. **I meet guys all the time who don't know how to grieve their way through the pain of divorce.** They are badly hurt, and many have a deep sense of shame, failure, and unbearable loss. Unable to grieve, they often end up hurting everyone around them, even their beloved children.

We need to learn how to grieve, to allow ourselves to be seen as "weak" and grieve our way through to clarity.

When I wrote those words only six months earlier, I had no idea that I would be one of those guys grieving my way through to clarity.

A short time later, a guy picked me up in his truck and took me not only to Auckland but went miles out of his way to get me where I needed to be. Legend!

That night, I did the **Nutters Club** radio show, which was great. The following day, Boris, the producer, who had kindly put me up at his house for the night, dropped me at a backpackers in the city.

I'd been talking to a journalist named Melanie Reid about the possibility of doing a story for a big NZ current affairs TV show called 3rd **Degree,** and during that day, it was all finalised. After Melanie met me and talked to her producers, we were a "go" to start shooting the following morning as I tried to hitch out of the city. This was the break I'd been waiting for. After all, the other half of this tour was about promoting the book and Wildman. This was a giant step in the right direction.

Up early the next morning, fridge packed, let's do this. This backpackers also had a flight of steps that I had managed to get my fridge down — just in time for Mel and her crew to show up and ask, "Could we get a shot of you getting the fridge down the steps?"

"Of course."

I pulled the fridge back up the steps and then back down. Damn, I was gonna look good naked after this tour with all of the workouts I'd had dragging the thing around.

We spent the morning getting the setup shots we needed, including me trying to hitch out of the city.

People stopped and chatted. Others bought books. A few people stopped but weren't going far enough. I needed to get to the far side of the motorway about an hour north, and I was willing to wait for it rather than get stranded on the motorway somewhere.

Finally, after a couple of hours, a familiar face pulled over. It was Rachel's cousin Maxine who I'd gotten to know a little over the years. What were the odds? She was heading north to visit her new grandchild and was more than happy to take me a little further to get me to the right spot.

I said goodbye to the film crew, who I would catch up with in a week or so on my way back through to finish the story, and I was off.

Maxine didn't know that Rachel and I had split, and it was actually really helpful talking it over with her as we headed north. She had been through a divorce a few years earlier, so it was good to get her perspective. When she dropped me off, she bought three of my books to give to different people before she gave me a big hug, and then off she went.

The following day, I was met once more with a scene straight out of a movie. A pickup truck came down the road towards me with what appeared to be a swarm of bees chasing it. As it got closer, it became apparent that it **was** a fucking swarm of bees! The truck pulled over right next to me.

"You want a lift?"

It turns out the owners of the vehicle had a couple of big blocks of beeswax on the back, which had attracted shitloads of bees. The bees were going hardcore, buzzing all around me and inside the vehicle as well. It didn't seem to bother them at all, or their baby, who was strapped into its car seat in the back!

Holy shit! Ya don't see that every day!

"Nah, I'm all good, thanks," I said. "I might just wait for something a little less 'beey.'"

My body thanked me as they drove off, bees in tow.

Later that day, as I unloaded the fridge from a ride, I noticed that one of the tyres on my sack trolley had split, and the inner tube was bulging out. This entire trip, I had carried a roll of duct tape inside the fridge like some kind of serial killer, and I finally had a purpose for it. I ripped it into eight-inch strips and placed the strips around the tyre from the inside over the tread and fixing it to the outside. I sat there for about half an hour doing my MacGyver repair until the masterpiece was complete—a masterpiece that lasted the rest of my journey.

I headed north to Awanui and decided I'd try to hit Pukenui for the night and base myself there to tackle Cape Reinga the (almost) northern most tip of NZ the following day.

The first guy pulled over. "I'm just heading to the Waipapakauri pub five minutes up the road. I can drop ya there if ya like."

"I might wait and see if I can get further," I said.

Then another car pulled up. "I'm just heading to the Waipapakauri pub."

"Popular place," I said.

A third car pulled up.

"Let me guess," I said. "You're heading to the Waipapakauri pub, right?"

"How did ya know that?" the driver asked.

"Lucky guess," I replied. Then I jumped in, and we headed

off to the pub.

It was a busy little pub in the middle of nowhere. I got myself a pint and chatted with the locals. Then I realised, shit, it was six o'clock, and I still had a long ride ahead of me—if I could even get a ride. So I finished my beer and headed across the road to try and find a safe place to stand.

The roads are really narrow that far north, because there isn't a lot of traffic, so to find a safe-ish place to stand where people could actually see me was a bit of a mission. To start with, I was right opposite the pub, but I started to feel a bit weird, because everyone across the road kept staring at me, talking amongst themselves, and then staring again. So I moved on. When I did find my spot, I stood there for about an hour before a kind and lovely lady picked me up and dropped me in Pukenui.

I rocked on up to the first place, but they had no vacancies. I pushed the fridge up the road to the next, and they were full, too. I'd carted my tent in the fridge for the whole trip and had never needed to use it—until then. Luckily, the people at the second place said I could pitch it there if I wanted. A feeling of relief washed over me, since I was completely fucked from the long day on the road.

A group of avocado pickers was staying there—tourists on

working holiday visas—and a couple of Aussie guys. Sorted!

The shops were closed by that time, so I couldn't contribute any alcohol to the group for the night's festivities.

"No worries, mate," said "Beard," one of the Aussie guys. "Just have a few of mine."

"I'll tell ya what, I'll trade ya one of my books for a few beers," I replied. He was pretty happy with that. I sat down, cracked one open, and joined in with the group for the night. Once again, as with most backpackers, the atmosphere was happy and relaxed. We drank and smoked the night away, telling stories and laughing 'til late.

The next morning, I was up and on the road by seven. It was only an hour's drive to the Cape, so I left my tent where it was, unpacked my fridge to make it easier for the day, and headed out.

I caught my first ride within the hour, a local who was working in the logging industry. He dropped me off twenty minutes north in a place that was, of course, in the middle of nowhere. Everywhere up there is the middle of nowhere.

From there north, the majority of vehicles were tourists heading to Ninety Mile Beach or the lighthouse at the Cape, so the next wait was a couple of hours or more. I didn't mind at all. The scenery up there is gorgeous, the sun was shining, and I was confident that at some point that day, I would hit the very top of New Zealand.

The next ride dropped me another twenty minutes north outside the last gas station, which didn't seem to be open or in operation.

The first people who pulled up to the station about twenty minutes later were a young British couple. I told them what I was doing and asked for a ride to the top. They were pretty keen to help if we could fit the fridge. Their car was a people mover that had the back seats down and converted into a bed. We lifted the fridge up on top of their bed with just enough room to clear it. However, it left very little room for me! I slid in next to the fridge, and there was only enough room for me to lie on my side spooning the fridge as they closed the back door and took off north.

The Cape!

I was squashed and slightly in pain by the time we hit the top, but it was awesome. I had done it!

They opened the back door, and I wriggled out, grabbed the fridge and stood there looking like I'd just conquered Everest or something.

A guy came up to me. "Hey, didn't I see you on the telly a couple of weeks ago?"

Then another guy who had passed me way down south a month earlier came up to talk.

"Wow, you're like really famous," the British guy who had just given me the ride said, looking very chuffed that he had been a part of my journey. I nodded with a big smile on my face, knowing full well that most people had absolutely no idea who I was. I hefted the fridge and pushed it down the big winding hill to the lighthouse.

It is such an amazing part of the country. I must have spent an hour or more just soaking in the place.

By that point, the car park was full, and I was feeling hopeful I'd get out of there by the end of the day.

An hour passed, no worries. Two hours. No worries? Three hours, and the car park was looking pretty empty. Shit! The one day I was about to get stranded, and I didn't have my tent or a sleeping bag or anything!

It was four in the afternoon, and only five vehicles were left in the car park. I started to look around for places I could sleep if things ended up going that way. Then someone appeared from the track and headed to their car.

Shit! That car won't fit the fridge!

Four cars left, and only two that could fit a fridge.

A little while later, another couple appeared and walked over to their vehicle. It was large enough to fit the fridge, if they were so inclined, so I rocked on up to them and asked if they would get me out of there.

They had seen me earlier in the day before heading off on a hike and were more than happy to take me back to Pukenui. I sooo wasn't stressed at all! Their vehicle was a brand new 4x4 that they had only owned for a week. Some people are really precious about new vehicles and would never allow a fridge to scuff it up a bit, but not these guys. Thank God!

By the time I got back to Pukenui, I'd been on the road for eleven hours. Eleven hours to do a two-hour return trip. I was making life hard for myself, but it was totally worth it.

I didn't stay up drinking with the avocado pickers. Once again, I was exhausted and headed off to bed early.

Over the next couple of days, I worked my way slowly, and I do mean *slowly,* south towards Auckland and then across to the Mount, where Lorena had found part-time work picking Kiwifruit. We booked two nights in a nice motel. Two nights turned into three, and we did nothing for those three days but make love, drink wine, and cook crepes naked (not recommended).

I'd never made love that much in my life. My entire life, I'd been envious of the stories of passion that others had shared, like I'd missed out on one of the greatest experiences life has to offer.

I'd always loved and cherished the fact that Rachel and I had only ever been with each other. I loved knowing that I was the only one who had ever fully experienced this beautiful woman, that she wasn't on anyone else's "list." But now, with that dream lost and sitting in ashes, I was going to experience all that life and love had to offer.

My mind was trapped between these two worlds, and for those three days, I lived in the tension of love, pleasure, discovery, pure elation and torment, grief and pain.

Lorena could feel it, too. She knew my story, but she did not sit in judgement of any of it. I was on a journey, as was she, and for the time we were together, it was exactly what we both needed. We held each other with an open hand, without expectation, just letting it be what it was for as long as it was.

It was really hard saying goodbye, as I hit the road for my final leg of the journey, not knowing if we would see each other again.

Rotorua, Taupo, Napier, I worked my way down country over the next few days. By the end of the week, I was home.

13

HOME TO AN EMPTY HOUSE

I walked in my front door that night to an empty house. I'd told Rachel to take the furniture and everything she needed for the kids. As I walked past my children's empty bedrooms, I was struck by an overwhelming wave of grief. I struggled to stand as the full extent of my loss hit home. I can't remember anything else from that night, but even now, two years later, those waves still hit me from time to time as I walk past my kids' bedrooms on the nights they're with their mother. It feels like part of me is missing.

The next couple of weeks leading up to Christmas were a blur as I got back into work and went shopping for bedding and plates and cups and basic kitchen stuff. One mate gave me a washing machine, and another gave me a dryer, but I still needed a fridge.

One night when my Wildman guys were over, I decided to plug in the fridge I'd used on tour. It was beaten and battered, having travelled upside down and sideways on nearly every form of transport imaginable over 4,500 km, but it was worth a crack, right?

We all gathered around, and with great trepidation, hoping not to get electrocuted, I plugged it in. From the silence came the beautiful humming sound of a healthy fridge.

"It fucking works!" I yelled with a huge grin on my face. What a legendary fridge.

I trolleyed it into my kitchen, plugged it back in, and it still runs today, the world's most travelled fridge covered in hundreds of signatures and messages from people I'd met on the road. It's a constant reminder of my madness, of the road less travelled, of cutting my own path through the wilderness of divorce.

Facing My First Christmas as a Broken Family

I wanted to stay amicable with Rach. I was hurt but not bitter, and I knew the best thing for the kids was for us to show respect towards each other. We may not love each other the same way anymore, but we could still act civilized.
I'm so glad neither of us is crazy. I've seen many people start to treat each other like shit after a breakup and try to control each other through the kids. This is often based in pain, hurt,

betrayal, or just because one or both are fucking crazy. The fridge tour had really helped me grieve deeply and find a sense of balance, and Rachel is generally a non-crazy type of person, so we were on good footing.

However, there was still pain, a fuck load of pain, such as when we tried to figure out the kids over the holiday season and how all of that was going to work. I was trying to work out when she was going away with the kids to be with her family so that I could find a small window to see Lorena.

"Can you guys please just figure it out so that I know what windows of time I have for my own plans?"

"What plans? Have you found someone else already?"

Women are so intuitive.

I'm not a liar, and, thinking back on it, I guess part of me just wanted her to know. Another part was feeling like, **We're all adults here. I've made an adult decision and shouldn't need to hide it.**

"I've moved on," I said.

Her face filled with pain. Oh fuck. I didn't want to do that. I hated seeing that. She had been my best friend for twenty years, and I didn't want to hurt her. I had moved on for me, to deal with my own pain and make a clean cut so I wouldn't pine after her, but whatever fleeting moment of not giving a fuck about her that I had experienced five seconds earlier was smashed to pieces when I saw the anguish in her face.

I was confused. We weren't together anymore, and there was no way we were getting back together. So, why not move on? I justified my actions over and over in my head.

"It's not like I left because I didn't love you and then found someone else. You didn't want me anymore, so what's the problem?" I verbalised my half-processed thoughts, which only added to the pile of shit.

What a fucking mess.

I didn't want to face my first Christmas in my house alone, and even though I would see my kids on Christmas morning, I would be facing Christmas Eve and the majority of Christmas Day without the love and laughter of my children. There was a deep cutting grief there. I would never have my kids as a full part of my life again. I would become a part-time dad, and they would be my part-time kids. No matter how many nights a week they stayed at my place, they would always leave. As a father who had poured my life into my children, this was the hardest part.

So, there I was, torn, trying to keep my head above the rising tide as my old and new worlds collided for the first time.

I called Lorena. "I don't think I can get away for a couple of days. I need to be the ex-husband Rachel needs me to be at the moment."

"That's okay. We're not teenagers anymore. We can wait."

Wow. This woman kept blowing me away with her love and understanding.

I let Rachel know, without spite or bitterness, that I'd put aside my tentative plans and would be there to work around her plans with her family.

Christmas Eve was a blur, but I think I popped over to see the kids before bed that night.

Christmas morning, however, I remember clearly. I was up at six thirty and over to Rachel's by seven to cook pancakes and open presents with the kids. It was surprisingly good. Yes, there was tension and a sense of brokenness, but we both managed to put that aside for the sake of the kids and had Christmas morning together like we always had before.

I left by ten, as Rachel was taking the kids to see her family for the next couple of days. I would drive out and join them the following day for a few hours, but until then I faced the rest of Christmas alone.

I got home and called Lorena to wish her a Merry Christmas. She was still hung over from the party the night before at the backpackers in Tauranga, and she relayed some of the wild stories.

I decided I needed to see this woman that day, because hearing her voice was driving me fucking crazy. So I jumped online and looked for flights from Tauranga to Wellington. I love living spontaneously, and it was such a rush even thinking of the possibility. Searching online . . . searching . . . Holy shit! A flight was leaving in just two hours!

She had just received an offer for work in the South Island the day before, so she needed to pass through Wellington anyway. I sent her the flight details.

"What do ya think?" I messaged her

Her reply: "I need to book the flight, have a shower, pack my bags, check out, and get to the airport within an hour on Christmas Day?"

I didn't hear anything for the next half hour. Was she going to do it or not? She was really hung over. Maybe she had just gone back to bed. I didn't know. I was starting to feel like that kid at Christmas who really hoped his parents had got him that new bike and was about to burst.

Then she sent me a text: "I've booked the flight and am standing outside the backpackers waiting for the taxi."

Holy shit! I'm getting my bike!

Twenty minutes later, another text: "The taxi still isn't here!"

No! I'm not getting my bike after all. I Googled frantically, trying to figure out how long it would take to get from the backpackers to the airport. What was the very latest she could check in and not miss her flight?

"19 minutes," I texted her, "that's all you've got."

"Taxi just arrived! I'm in the taxi!"

"Awesome! Okay, it's a 15 minute drive so when you get there you are going to have to run to make it! ☺"

I was sitting on the edge of my seat.

Fifteen, seventeen, nineteen minutes . . . I hadn't heard

anything. Had she made it? Twenty-one minutes. . . .
"I made it! I'm coming to see you!"

Oh, sweet Jesus! I'm a believer! You have no idea of the endorphin rush that hit me at that moment!

An hour and a half later, I was at the airport. As she walked towards me with that gorgeous smile, I couldn't believe how beautiful she was and what a lucky man I was to share some time with her.

Movie airport scene—French girl, the embrace, the kiss. Perfect.

We arrived back at my place and made love for the rest of Christmas Day. It was not the Christmas I had been expecting. It was beyond words.

Boxing Day.

I drove out of town and spent half the day with my kids and some of their cousins at a mate's place. BBQ, swimming pool. Kiwi Christmases are great that way, and I loved spending the time with my kids.

Later that afternoon, I returned home to Lorena, who wasn't due to leave on the ferry for another day.

I was struggling not to fall in love; we both were. I was feeling so many emotions that I hadn't felt in years and others I had never experienced. I felt like a teenager again, in love for the first time, and all of the passion mixed with the insecurity that goes with that.

I had to continue holding her with an open hand, like a butterfly that had landed gently in my palm. As long as my hand stayed open, it would be perfect for the time it was. If I tried to hold onto it, I would destroy it. "Open hand, Rob, open hand," was my mantra to keep my sanity.

We kept reminding ourselves that it was only for a time, a holiday romance. She would be heading back to Europe before long, and there was no way I was ready to be in a relationship no matter how perfect our time together was.

I only saw her one more time after that. We spent five nights together in Punakaiki and then, by mutual agreement, went our separate ways. Even so, she ended up being a bigger part of my story than I ever expected. Now that she's back home in Europe, we remain great friends.

14

"I DON'T MISS ANYTHING."

As I slipped into my new life over the next few months, one that involved having my beautiful kids for three nights a week, I started to find my feet again. I kept waiting to fall into deep depression, but it never came. I started wondering if I was fooling myself, that I wasn't allowing myself to feel the full extent of my loss, that I was in denial. But I wasn't, and I never hit that dark place I thought was inevitable. Pain yes, but not depression, and not the numbness that comes with that.

I did grieve a lot, and there were many nights when I drank myself to sleep. The drink also helped me to sob deeply. Sometimes my whole body convulsed with pain, but that was part of my healing.

I continued to process everything through with my Wildman group, and then one day it hit me. I was over at Rachel's house collecting the kids and having a bit of fun when I let a fart slip.

"I don't miss that," Rachel commented.

"I don't miss anything," was my instant reply. It sounded mean, but I wasn't trying to be.

"Neither do I," was her honest reply. We looked at each other. How was that possible after being together for so long? But it was true.

I didn't miss anything about my marriage, and there was nothing I wanted back. What's more, I wasn't nearly as lonely as I was when I was married. Marriage can be a lonely place once the connection is gone. There I was, four nights a week in an empty house without any new women on the scene, and instead of feeling lonely, I loved it.

I started to see it like this: You have a group of friends you've always known and always hung out with. If that's all you've ever experienced, that's all you know. Then one day you move and leave those friends behind, and you realise your view of friendship and what's normal is very limited, very narrow. While it may have been good at the time, there's a whole world of new friends and possibilities to explore.
Another thing I really loved was being a full-time solo dad for three days a week. My house, my rules.

On most Sunday mornings, I would take my kids to the

Wellington waterfront for a few hours. They would scooter around, we would buy food from the markets, and then usually end up at the beach. My kids would swim in their clothes even in mid-winter, and we wouldn't have any towels or spare clothes to change into. They would strip off and then scooter half-naked around the bay as we found our car.

That's the job of dads, isn't it? To give our children wings, to let them explore and just be kids. They were wild and free but still disciplined. I have a rule that if anyone stops listening to me, then we all go home, and I stick to it. Freedom within boundaries. I saw many dads who were at the beach with their partners looking at me with envy that I was being so relaxed with my kids. I felt relaxed. Life was good.

After the three nights, I had four days to recover before I got back into it again.

It was hard on the kids though. Their mum's house and then mine, over and over. This is the pain I never wanted them to go through, but I talked to them about it constantly and helped them process it.

I've always talked to my kids as if they were adults. Kids understand a lot more than we think. I didn't hide anything from them; whatever they wanted to talk about, we talked about. I allowed them to truly see me. I didn't hide my pain, didn't put on a happy mask. I taught them that it's okay to go through something painful, that this is normal, and the best way to deal with it is to talk and process.

"Are you and mum ever getting back together?"

"No, son, we're not."

"Why not?"

"We don't love each other in that way anymore, but we both still really love you! And to be honest, son, I don't know what I'm doing. I've never been through a divorce before. I'm just trying to figure it out as I go along, and that's okay."

"I love you, Dad."

Teaching my kids raw, brutal honesty won't just set them up well for when the storms of life hit. I also hope that this modelling will mean that, as they get older, they will see me as someone they can approach and with whom they can process life.

15

SIGNS, SEX, AND WONDERS

As much as I love my own company, I also really enjoy the company of women, so with my four free nights a week, I started going out on the town. I even took up Ceroc dancing and loved it.

Because I was so religious when I was a teen and then married young, I missed a big part of what many people experience. It seemed like I was going in the opposite direction of everyone else my age. Whilst others were settling down and becoming more spiritual, I was rediscovering my youthful exuberance. Even so, I never felt the need to push the envelope like many do when they're young, one of the benefits I suppose of having a few more years of experience under my belt. I went out a lot, but I never got fucked up. I just seemed to find balance.

During that time, I was working as a builder on Courtney Place in Wellington, which seems to have an exceptionally high rate of gorgeous women. All day every day, streams of these ladies walked past our construction site.

I felt like I was at one of those sushi train bars where the sushi glides by on the little track, but my hands were unable to grab one. Twenty years without use, and only recently trying to get my arms moving again. I was really hungry, and the primal need to sow my wild oats was kicking in big time.

I didn't like the idea of online dating. It was so foreign to me. It seemed weird and a little desperate, maybe a little impersonal. I liked the idea of just meeting people, feeling the chemistry, and going from there. But I was still working on that skillset, still trying to get my arms moving, without much luck. Part of me was also concerned about what Rachel would think if I went online. Strangely enough, what she thought still mattered to me, especially if I was coming across as lame or desperate. It's amazing the power we give other people sometimes, living out of fear of what others think rather than just living.

So, I took matters into my own hands. I wrote signs and started to put them out on the street.

"Builder requires date for tonight, apply within (guys need not apply)"

The above ground breaking sign was my reaction to a good mate of mine, Derek, who I've known since I was four, asking me out on a man date. As much as I love hitting the town with him, I was looking to spend time with someone without a penis.

The sign had a lot of people stopping and laughing, but it didn't produce any results, so a man date with Derek that night it was.

The following week I put out another sign.

"Friday is international Make Love to a Builder Day!
(Don't feel foolish on Monday morning at work because you missed it)
Guys still need not apply."

Once more, my sign got a lot of attention, and I'd pop outside periodically to talk to people and point the sign out to gorgeous women who may have missed it. By Friday, I'd made the back page of our national newspaper and was all over Facebook, but I still hadn't secured a date.

The following week, I had my next sign out. "Offline dating" followed by a profile of my awesomeness and what qualities I desired in a woman. Once again, my sign made the back page of the national paper, and now women were poking their heads into the construction site asking for me.

One day, there seemed to be a lack of women popping in to say hello, and upon further investigation, I discovered that Greenpeace had moved into the neighbourhood for the day to gather signatures, and they were doing so right in front of my sign. I went out and politely asked the guy to move down the road a few meters so he wouldn't obstruct my sign. He was apologetic and moved on. However, within a short time he was back. After this occurred several times throughout the day I had no other choice but to picket Greenpeace. I wrote another sign.

"Greenpeace is ruining my dating life"

I proceeded to follow around the well-intended but slightly annoying young volunteer protesting and picketing his chosen place to stand. This may have been the highlight of my life.

The following day, things were back to normal. In fact, it got to the point where my workmate Jason, tired of been asked if he was Rob, got some T-shirts made up: "I am not Rob" for himself and "I am Rob" for me.

I started having loads of off-the-cuff coffee dates at the café next door. I was learning quickly about chemistry and reading body language whilst practising my flirting and conversation skills.

I set up a Facebook page to start a conversation about intimacy, connection, and sex. I would blog and then get feedback from different women on the topics posted. My entire paradigm was shifting as my beliefs around sex and love were challenged and stretched.

I started being more honest with myself about what I really wanted at that moment in time, and although deep down the desire for intimacy was huge, I also just wanted to go wild and fuck. As soon as I was honest with myself—and the women I met—I started getting laid. It sounds a little crass writing it that way, but that's how it was.

16

FRENCH GIRL NEEDED TO HITCHHIKE WITH FRIDGE

At that time, I was still working on my charity, Project Wildman, but my energy was floundering. I'd set Wildman up back in a time when I had all my basic needs covered and, therefore, had excess energy to pour into it. When I started, my marriage and family were intact, as were my home and finances. Slowly, each of these things had been stripped away through my own doing and the hand of others, and I was in a place where I didn't have the emotional strength required to carry it on. I kept trying, and I even managed to get Wildman set up and running in Christchurch and Auckland, but I was fading fast, and I couldn't put in the effort needed to grow and maintain it. All of that hard work I'd poured into it over the past few years, and now it was falling away.

I started planning the second fridge tour, which ended up being a mixture of things. I really wanted and needed to hit the road again for my own mental health, to get more of my mojo back, and I wanted to see Wildman grow, but deep down I knew I no longer had what it needed. A year into my separation, and I was still healing from my world tipped on its head.

I set a goal of fundraising $24,000 to get Wildman set up in more centres throughout the country. My team got behind me and organised speaking engagements as I went.

I hit the road in early November, just like I had done the previous year. This time I got free ferry passage and was allowed to take the fridge on board in the main passenger area. The first fridge was still in use in my kitchen. This fridge, "Steve," had been donated by one of our members and was duly named after him.

On board the ferry, I wrote a sign to go on Steve:

"French girl needed to hitchhike with fridge"

"Does she need to be French?" I heard an Italian voice say.

I turned around to see this beautiful woman. "No," I said. "Italian's good."

"I'm travelling with a French girl. Want to meet her?"

"Okay, that sounds good, too."

Giulia (pronounced "Julia") was the Italian beauty. Her lovely French friend was Cindy (pronounced "Cindy" ☺).

Okay, so this was a pretty fucking awesome start to my tour! I spent some time chatting with them, and it turned out they were heading to Paradiso in Nelson for the night, the same hostel that had nearly ended me the year before. Now I had a goal for the day. I had to reach Nelson by nightfall! Charity? What charity? Focus, Rob, focus!

I headed back to the fridge and started talking to Josie from Ireland. I loved her accent and Irish charm, and we flirted away for a while before exchanging details in the hopes of catching up somewhere down the west coast, which we inevitably did.

The ferry pulled into Picton, and I was off! There was no way I wasn't getting to Nelson that night. With the speed of the gods behind me, by six o'clock, I was there!

I checked in, walked through to the dining room, and there they were.

"You made it!" they exclaimed.

"Hell yeah I made it!"

I recounted the stories of the day on the road, and then we spent all night talking, laughing, and drinking wine.
Later that night, I found myself walking with Giulia over to the old bus that was set up as a movie room. A group of young guys were there watching football, and Giulia and I found a quiet place to sit away from the others.

As soon as we sat down, I turned and kissed her. Sometimes in life you just get the perfect kiss back. We were lost in each other. When the guys left, we ended up with the whole bus to ourselves. I could feel the pace of where she was at, and we kept things at that level for the rest of the night, just kissing, being intimate, connecting.

"Just kissing." It's interesting reflecting on this as I write, because kissing is such an intimate thing, and there are times, like that night with Giulia, when it is so good and so perfect that I prefer it to fucking. Did I really just say that? Yes, I did.

The following day, I went out and did some media—local TV, newspapers, and so on—as I had on the previous tour, before taking on my first speaking engagement that night. Only two guys showed up. Can't say I wasn't disappointed, but in the end, those two guys were totally worth the effort and resulted in me talking to a large group of guys the following day before I hit the road.

Still in Nelson on the second night, I returned to the backpackers, where Giulia and Cindy where just returning from a day of hiking and exploring.

As the night went on, I asked Giulia if she'd like to come over to my room for a few hours. I was in a four-bed dorm, and my bed was a double up on top of a single. We headed to my room, and what I thought would be another night of sensual kissing became a night of intense passion as the German girl on the bunk below tried to block out the noise.

17

GUINNESS WORLD RECORD

On my first tour when I was about a third of the way through, I received a call from my mate Hamish. "You must be close to breaking the world record for the furthest distance hitchhiking with a fridge."

"There's a record?"

It turns out that Tony Hawks, who inspired my first fridge escapade, was in the *Guinness Book of World Records* for traveling with a fridge.

"What's the record?"

"One thousand six hundred and fifty kilometers."

"Shit, I'll triple that by the time I'm done, and my fridge is three times bigger—not that size matters of course."

However, I hadn't documented any of my travels, except through the odd Facebook post. This time 'round, I was going to do it right. Everyone who picked me up signed my form and wrote where they had taken me from and to. By the end, I'd travelled 4,732 km (2940.32 miles). For the past year all that paperwork has been sitting on my desk ready to be finished and sent in to claim my title. Fuck. Okay, add to the list of things to do before publishing book.

In the first thirteen drafts of this book, I didn't put the following piece in. I never even wrote it, but reading through it for the last time, it feels incomplete without it.

Setting up Wildman made me feel like I had finally achieved something great, that I'd found something deeply fulfilling to which I could dedicate my life. But the second fridge tour was almost a confirmation that I was slowly losing that, too.

My team of guys were organising all my speaking events as I went along, including the necessary media and advertising. They poured so much into it; we all did. However, on many occasions after a long hard day on the road, I'd arrive at the venue and find only one or two guys had shown up.

Our fundraising was also struggling. By the halfway mark, I'd only raised around $2,000 of the $24,000 for which I'd hoped. Everyone was working so hard, but it just wasn't happening. Needless to say, my enthusiasm was dying fast.

But we also had some great nights, and by the end, I had six more cities where there were enough guys amping to get Wildman set up and running. Brilliant! Except for the fact that donating towards men removing masks and talking is not really a big heartstring puller. Mix that with the all or nothing structure with which we had chosen to fundraise, and by the end, we had raised zero. Six cities ready to go, and I had no time or money to help get them set up.

The next few months after the tour, I talked to my guys and expressed that I had nothing left to give. No matter how much I wanted to keep pushing, I was empty.

However, still on tour and struggling massively in one area did not mean I wasn't going to try and have some fun. So, towards the end of the tour as I had done at the beginning, that's exactly what I did. No need for everything to be so fucking depressing right?

I'd decided to take Steve on a few adventures along the way, including getting a ride in one of New Zealand's smallest cars, (a shortened, convertible Mini Cooper), dolphin watching, and an unsuccessful attempt to paddle board him in the ocean. It was in Paihia towards the top of the North Island while attempting some of these antics that I met Kathrin from Germany.

I'd booked into the hostel and was standing at my new bunk wondering why the floor was all wet when her voice exclaimed, "Don't you know? This is the pee room!"

Hmm . . . okay. The story goes that the night before, an American guy, as drunk as a drunk thing, mistook a girl in her bunk as a toilet and just opened up on her. The American guy was so embarrassed the following morning that he grabbed his stuff and ran, and the girl was so stressed she asked to be transferred to another room. The whole experience had created a strangely strong bond with the rest of the dorm.

So, there I was, with this now close-knit group of travellers, brought together by what is not as rare an event as one would hope, and I hit it off with all of them instantly. We hung out, cooked, and ate together. It was brilliant. The whole time though I was looking at Kathrin thinking, *You're pretty fucking amazing.* Not only was she gorgeous, she was so full of life, with the biggest laugh in the world. One of those people whose energy is so contagious that I just need to be around them. But, soon enough, my time there came to an end. We all said goodbye, and off I headed.

A week later, I hit the Cape and had picked up a ride all the way down to Auckland when I got a message from her.

"I'm in Whangarei. Where are you?"

"Just about to head through Whangarei on my way to Auckland."

"There's room at the backpackers if you want to come here."

My plans changed immediately. I was there in an hour.

I think she just liked my company and wasn't looking for anything else. In fact, we had had that conversation, and I told her I'd stop hitting on her for the day, but if I stayed another night, I probably wouldn't be able to control myself.

It was a small but lively group at the hostel that night, and I found myself and another guy belting out some songs on the guitar. I've sang since I was a teen, but only recently had I learned the guitar. Most of the songs I'd learned were love ballads, not for any particular reason other than that I loved to sing them, and they had been a big part of the previous year's healing process.

Kathrin was especially partial to one song, "Iris," by the Goo Goo Dolls. Over the course of the night, she kept asking me to sing it, and, naturally, I obliged.

Later that night as I headed off to bed, she came into our dorm with the guitar in hand and asked me to play it one more time.

Now, the guy who wrote the lyrics for this song is a lyric god! *"'Cause I'd give up forever to touch you, 'cause I know that you feel me somehow. . . . "* and on it goes.

After I played, I looked over at her in her bed. "Ya know, it's just wrong for two really ridiculously good looking people to sleep in different beds. I think it's somehow fucking up the universe... sooo, It's probably best if you come over here. I think that would help put everything back in order again."

After a bit more toing and froing, she got up, locked the door, and headed over. We had an incredible night together.

The following night, we snuck into the empty room next door. Then, at twelve o'clock, right in the middle of some spectacular moves, someone banged on the door.

"It's Dorothy. Who's in there?"

She was the owner and a lovely lady, but she did not sound happy.

"It's Rob. Can you just give me a few minutes?"

"I've got people checking in, and I'm not impressed!"

Fuck!

We looked at each other and jumped up. Our clothes were scattered everywhere. We scrambled to find them, hurriedly getting dressed and trying to straighten the place out a bit before opening the door. We felt like teenagers who had been caught by her parents fucking on the couch.

We sat on the steps outside of the kitchen and waited for Dorothy to finish checking the new people in before she came to see us. As she crossed the floor towards us, the biggest, cheekiest grin came over her face.

"Who the hell checks in at twelve o'clock at night?" she exclaimed.

Oh sweet relief! We spent one more night together, and then the next day Kathrin flew home to Germany. As Lorena had done a year earlier, Kathe had stolen a piece of my heart.

This is the thing about holiday romances: you only get the good bits, the romance, the love. It's absolutely perfect with none of the day-to-day grind of a real relationship. It's so intoxicating and so very hard to let go of.
Over the next couple of months, we messaged each other

constantly until it was finally time to let go.

18

TINDERELLA — WILD OATS AND LOVE

I was still years away from even the thought of truly falling in love and all that goes along with that. The previous year had opened my eyes to so much, and I was hungry.

I'd resisted online dating for so long, but one day I finally decided it was time. I chose Tinder, because it was quickest and easiest to set up, and it was well known as a hook-up app. Perfect.

I started playing, and before long figured out that I didn't really enjoy the whole meeting a stranger for a drink idea. Was I witty, charming, or sexy enough? It was a lot of pressure when all I actually wanted, now that I was being honest with myself, was to get laid. So I decided to change my tack. I would only use it to get women straight into bed. No dating or strings attached, just sex.

It went against everything I'd ever believed about love,

romance, and sex, but I felt it was an important part of my journey, to just go out and be wild and explore a very raw sexual side of myself that I had never tapped into before. I was willing to give it a good try anyway ☺.

Because I am a lover, I think and dream like a lover. So I started messaging women as just that. I became a Mills and Boon style writer and began painting fine pictures of the erotic things I'd do to them—slow, sensual kissing, touching, and laying them gently on the bed… passion mixed with deep desire. I learned through trial and error how to arouse a woman in such a way that she would be willing to drive for hours or even fly from the other end of the country to spend a night with me.

At that stage, I was working in Napier as a builder by day and then, a few nights a week, throwing oats around into the early hours, often getting only a couple of hours' sleep. At the end of each week, I travelled the four hours back to Wellington to have my children for the weekend before doing it all over again, week after week.

Meeting these beautiful women was like a dream. For some it was pure lust and an entire box of condoms thrashed before the night was done. With others it was a slow dance doused in intimacy and connection but never allowing myself to connect enough to get hurt. Others pushed my boundaries, and I discovered some stuff I'm just not into!

I learned so much, my eyes were fully opened, and I wanted more and more and more. Then Kiri entered my world and changed everything.

Kiri.

We'd matched through a series of events. She lived in Auckland, and I lived in Wellington, but I was still working in Napier. I knew exactly how I wanted this scene to play out. Seducing her with my words, which were playful yet deeply erotic in tone and tempo, I set the scene as to what I would do to her. I wanted to meet Kiri in a beautiful room, for her to arrive first, for me to enter, walk straight up to her, kiss her, and on it would go.

She was intrigued but cautious. "I've never been kissed like that before. . . . How do I know you won't kill me?"

"I'll make it quick," I replied.

She Googled me and asked for a live picture, even going as far as doing a police check as she crossed off her safety list. I continued to seduce her, loving the chase, loving this world of endless possibilities.

Then one day I received the message for which I'd been hoping. "I've booked a flight."

She was in. This was her first time ever to do something crazy like this, but I'd lit a fire inside of her that couldn't be quenched. I booked a beautiful waterfront room. A week later, she arrived, taxied to the hotel, and settled in.

I finished work early, went to my place, and got myself ready. Then headed down the road to the hotel.

"I'm here," I messaged. "Let me know when you're ready."

No reply. I waited in the car park, not wanting to enter her space until she was ready. Ten minutes passed. Nothing.

Then: "The door's unlocked."

I walked upstairs to the second floor, knocked, and entered. I looked across the room, the balcony doors wide open, the wild ocean crashing in the background, the wind blowing the curtains, and there in the midst of it all stood the most gorgeous woman. Was I in a movie again? Wow.

I put my bag down and looked at her across the room. "Hi."

"Hi," she replied, with her gown blowing in the breeze and

her big Dianna Ross hair.

I crossed the room towards her. "This is crazy, eh?"

"Yeah, a little bit."

I walked straight up to her and gave her the kiss I'd promised, that slow gentle approach where our lips barely meet, my lips moving across her cheek to her neck.

The woman in my arms was strong and powerful; everything about her told me so. But the look in her eyes was one of complete surrender and vulnerability. My kiss had confirmed that I was exactly what and who I said I was, a lover, and she trusted me with her all.

We kissed slowly there in the balcony doorway, exploring each other gently with our touch. Moving to the bed, we made love, hour after hour. Our time was made even more surreal by moments of deep conversation and connection. We shared jokes and laughed 'til our sides hurt, drank wine, and grazed on delicious food. I pulled out my guitar and sang her a few songs as she relaxed in the Jacuzzi. It was nothing short of perfect.

We continued throughout the night. In the morning, I dropped her at the airport, but it wasn't a drop and run "see ya later" deal. I walked her in, we had breakfast together, and then we stood there in the middle of the airport surrounded by people, holding each other and kissing like we were long-lost lovers parting ways once more.

Okay, I wasn't expecting that, I thought as Kiri took up residency inside my head.

A week later, I was in Auckland. I hadn't had a weekend off in four months, and now I was in Kiri's city with four nights planned together.

She was waiting at the airport when I arrived. Fuck, she was gorgeous. We kissed like those long-lost lovers once more as all the noise and busyness of the airport went quiet.

Those four days were filled with passion, love, laughter, arm wrestling in cafes, and cartwheel competitions in the middle of the mall, where we stopped and asked complete strangers to judge us. We had a deep connection that neither of us could deny. Fuck! I really wasn't ready for that. I needed at least another couple more years, didn't I? At my core was a man who just wanted to connect and experience true intimacy, but I didn't feel like I was ready. There was still so much to experience, so many adventures to have, but also a deep, hidden fear of being hurt again.

That week back in Napier, I spent a couple of nights with different women. It was good, but it wasn't the same. Something was missing. This "fucking" was no longer anywhere near enough.

Kiri, in the meantime, also feeling a deep connection but not wanting to just be another number, cut things off. It hurt like fuck, but I couldn't go there. I couldn't risk the pain of loving and losing.

One of the women I was with that week, whom I'd spent time with before, knew I'd been away for four nights in Auckland and asked me about my weekend.

"It was amazing," I replied.

"So, what are you going to do about it?" she asked.

"Nothing," I said. "I'm not ready. I'm not seeing her again."

"Are you kidding me? You're not ready? That's a bit weak."

I didn't like hearing that, but she was right. I had a lot of soul searching to do, and I was thrown head-first into mental crisis. I mean, another woman who really liked me and wanted to take it further was pointing out, to the detriment of herself, how I shouldn't let Kiri go. Fuck! That's some really fucked-up shit.

I took some time, wrote a list of what I wanted and needed in a woman, and Kiri ticked all the main boxes. She was vivacious, truly alive, raw and authentic, gorgeous, intelligent, fun, funny, passionate, generous, ambitious, and she took responsibility for her own life. Add to that the unbelievable sex, and there was nothing lacking. It was so good. And the way she looked at me, no one has ever looked at me like that before. Her vulnerability and willingness to be seen completely by me was intoxicating.

She had deleted me from Facebook and maybe from her cell phone. I wasn't sure, but I messaged her, not knowing if she had blocked my number or not.

Then she called me back. Yes! I wasn't blocked. We started messaging again, a phone call, more messages, but I still couldn't get my head and heart around a relationship.

"Fuck it, I'm coming to see you," she messaged me.

"No way! I'm not going to cause you any more pain." So valiant of me to make it look like I was protecting her.

"Okay."

And then I messaged her the other half of the story. "I would love to spend another four, eight . . . a hundred nights in your arms, but how close would we be then? I don't want to fall for you any more than I already have. I can't stand the pain of knowing that one day it will end. I'm not willing to risk being hurt again yet. I need a couple more years. Aaaaaaarrrrrhhhh! But I really want you! This sucks!"

Her reply was short and to the point. "Delete me!"

My head was spinning. "Meeting you has thrown me head-first into a fucking tumultuous crisis where I have a lot of soul searching to do! Fuck!!!"

She sent another message: "Stop beating yourself up. Stay honest and true to your path xxx. I have fallen for you, too!"

Fuck, she was awesome. That night I looked deep inside, and the following morning, I messaged her again.

"Hi."

"Is it 2017 yet?" Her brilliant reply.

"Maybe. . . . "

"Want to jump on my couch and watch some YouTube?"

"Would love to! Cartwheels and arm wrestling?"

"Ha-ha yup, that's how we roll!"

"Do you have a plan for the Wellington/Auckland distance thing?"

"I have thought about buying my own plane. Would that work?"

By the end of that day, I had deleted my Tinder account and let everyone know I was no longer available. I was in, boots and all.

I let my walls down and allowed myself to fall in love. The woman who had been consuming my thoughts for the past month was now mine, and as amazing as that was, it was also terrifying. This was not a woman who would be flying back to Europe tomorrow so that I could risk feeling these deep feelings because she was leaving and that somehow made it safe. Kiri was right in front of me.

For the next few weeks, I did constant mental checks, asking myself hard questions to make sure I was fully awake and not just off in La La Land. Was I really ready for this? Could one ever truly be ready? Was I choosing this out of fear? Fear of what? What did I love most about Kiri? What aspects of her personality and life did I find challenging and which I was afraid would drive me fucking crazy? Were they deal-breakers or not? What was negotiable, and what wasn't? What were personality traits, and what were learned behaviours, responses, and reactions?

I don't have a problem with over thinking things (denial). Fuck, I just really didn't want to get hurt.

Question after question on both sides as we learned more about each other. We had fallen for each other in a passionate way, but we also had the life experiences and skills to navigate our way through areas that would make for a very explosive relationship otherwise. We were honest and set boundaries with each other, pointing out old bruises and areas on which we should tread lightly. But even this, as I was about to find out, is not a guarantee. Sometimes bruises mask giant wounds lying just beneath the surface.

We had spent some amazing time together, Kiri flying to Napier and me flying to Auckland, with all of our in-between time spent on the phone or FaceTiming. Then one night on the phone, I gently touched something that I knew was a bruise on Kiri's heart, a bruise that turned out to be a deep, gaping wound. Her response was silence as she processed it, a silence that grew more and more unbearable as the night wore on. I tried to distract myself from it, to give her the space she needed, but her silence screamed in my head. Had I given my heart to someone who would now jump all over it? Why wasn't she talking? Was it that bad? On and on my overactive and now insecure mind went.

I hardly slept a wink. In the morning, I sent her a message and waited to hear her confirm what I'd already built up in my mind as the end of our short-lived relationship.

A little while later, I received a reply. Her text was angry and cold, at least by my standards. It was followed by a call. On the other end of the phone was a very intelligent and quick-witted woman who was hurt, and I couldn't get anything I wanted to say across without being met with sharpness. Exhausted from lack of sleep and feeling totally steamrolled, I burst into tears like an eleven-year-old girl. Where the fuck was all this raw emotion coming from? I was in deep pain, and as soon as she heard that, she softened. Unable to compose myself, I hung up. She called back, but I couldn't answer. I was a complete mess. What the fuck was this?

And then it hit me—I was lying in the same spot in the same room in which my wife had ended our marriage two years earlier. This wasn't just Kiri's wound but the fact her wound was pressing so hard on mine.

For the previous two years, I had avoided deep connection,

because I didn't want to feel that again, and now there I was.

I messaged her to let her know I couldn't talk yet, and she messaged back asking if I could just listen. She called again, and I answered as wave upon wave of emotion hit me. As embarrassing as all this crying was, I was also proud that I'd allowed myself to go there rather than using anger to protect myself, as I'd done in the past. I also realised I trusted Kiri enough to allow myself to truly be seen by her: no walls, no defences. When she hit me, I bled raw authenticity.

I had just seen a very hard side of Kiri, but I was about to see one of the softest and most beautiful sides, too, as she saw me in pain and reached out with a healing hand.

Over the next few weeks, I learned many lessons on trying to make something work when both parties have so much past pain and baggage. How to stay connected while at the same time trying to navigate through unrealistic expectations and bruises and all that comes with trying to build a new relationship.

Love, passion, sex, connection, boundaries, bruises, negotiating, pizza, wine, love languages, and long distance. With touch being such a strong love language for both of us, the long distance thing started to take its toll, and the gorgeous woman I'd fallen for was slowly disappearing as hidden walls were constructed.

I became so lost. My head was spinning constantly. It felt like a fuzzy cloud had moved into where my mind once sat. I had no idea which way was up or down. Where was the woman with whom I'd fallen in love? I was met with wall after wall. I could see the gold, her tenderness, her gentleness, and her all-encompassing loving side. It was there when I approached her slowly across the kitchen floor, when I kissed and held her, and when we made love, but the rest of the time it was locked away, and it tormented me.

Then, on the night of my forty-second birthday in a beautiful room on Waiheke Island Kiri had booked for us, I ended it. I should have known by then to stay away from birthdays and anniversaries.

I sat on the bed beside her. "I don't know how to love you the way you need to be loved. I don't think I'm the right man for you." I talked on in a calm and gentle tone that was full of love, honesty and pain.

It must have been the best break-up in the history of break-ups. We talked and laughed and loved for one last night while at the same time allowing ourselves to feel just how painful it was. We really did love each other.

Maybe we weren't ready for this love, or maybe we just let pain and the fear of loss win at the end of the day. As we continued to talk and stay close for some weeks to come, I saw that tender, vulnerable, and gorgeous side of Kiri again as she talked of her own journey through life and love.

We may not be together, but she still holds a massive piece of my heart. Without her, I would not have learned that even though things don't always work out, it's still safe to love again.

Back home, I stood once more in front of my fridge, reflecting on just how far I'd come over the past couple of years from my first days standing on the side of the road, broken.

On top of my fridge sat a half finished bottle of vodka. **One last time and then I'm done with you,** I thought to myself as I poured a drink, lit a cigarette, grabbed my guitar, and headed out into the sun.

There has been no manual to this journey of mine, and most days I have no fucking idea what I'm doing. But my curiosity about life and love will get me there one day.

Always end with a good quote, but never the same as the opening quote.

Fuck it.

"The reason we struggle with insecurity is because we compare our behind-the-scenes with everyone else's highlight reel." **Steve Furtick**

My highlight reel, like most people's, is fucking spectacular.

But it's been the behind-the-scenes everyday life and learning to deal with all the good, the bad, and the ugly that life throws at me that has created the real gold. My true "highlight reel" was forged through blood and tears, and most have never seen it. I can't put it up on Facebook, because it's my character and the man I've become.

Oh, to have the courage to truly be seen—that is our gold.

33241878R00106

Made in the USA
Middletown, DE
05 July 2016